100 BEST POEMS

for Children

PUFFIN BOOKS

Published by the Penguin Group
Penguin Books Ltd, 80 Strand, London WC2R 0RL, England
Penguin Group (USA), Inc., 375 Hudson Street, New York, New York 10014, USA
Penguin Books Australia Ltd, 707 Collins Street, Melbourne, Victoria 3008, Australia
Penguin Books Canada Ltd, 10 Alcorn Avenue, Toronto, Ontario, Canada M4V 3B2
Penguin Books India (P) Ltd, 11 Community Centre, Panchsheel Park, New Delhi – 110 017, India
Penguin Group (NZ), cnr Airborne and Rosedale Roads, Albany, Auckland 1310, New Zealand
Penguin Books (South Africa) (Pty) Ltd, Block D, Rosebank Office Park,
181 Jan Smuts Avenue, Parktown North, Gauteng 2193, South Africa

Penguin Books Ltd, Registered Offices: 80 Strand, London WC2R 0RL, England

puffinbooks.com

First published by Viking 2001
Published in Puffin Books 2002
018

The Acknowledgements on pages 136 to 138 constitute an extension of this copyright page

The moral right of the illustrator has been asserted

Manufactured in China

British Library Cataloguing in Publication Data
A CIP catalogue record for this book is available from the British Library

ISBN-13: 978–0–141–31058–9

100 BEST POEMS

for Children

Chosen by Children Edited by Roger McGough

Illustrated by Sheila Moxley

PUFFIN BOOKS

INTRODUCTION

P utting together an anthology, though pleasurable, is an onerous task. It involves reading every other decent anthology (not to find poems, but rather to make sure yours doesn't duplicate and re-present what is already in print). And then there is the exciting part, the trawl through bookshelves and bookshops on the lookout for new poems and new poets. It is a great feeling when it's over and a thrill when the book finally appears, by which time your compiler is invariably verse-drunk, and wary of taking on a similar commission for the next twenty years.

However, when invited by Philippa Milnes-Smith at Puffin Books to edit a 100 Best Poems for Children, my hangover magically disappeared as I leaped once more into the rhythmic fray. For in this case, it was the teachers and children of 135 schools up and down the country who did the reading and the choosing. They responded enthusiastically to a questionnaire sent out from Puffin to nominate their favourite poems in three categories: contemporary, more than 25 years old, and more than 100 years old. Over 280 nominations rolled in and the hundred most popular are to be found within. Some new poems, bursting with pride, and some classics, old hands at appearing in anthologies, pleased to be included, but not smug. My thanks to all concerned.

Roger McGough

CONTENTS

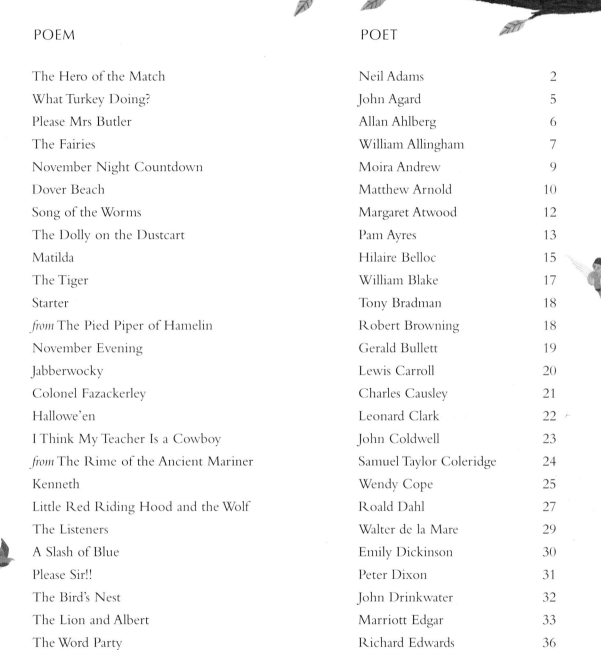

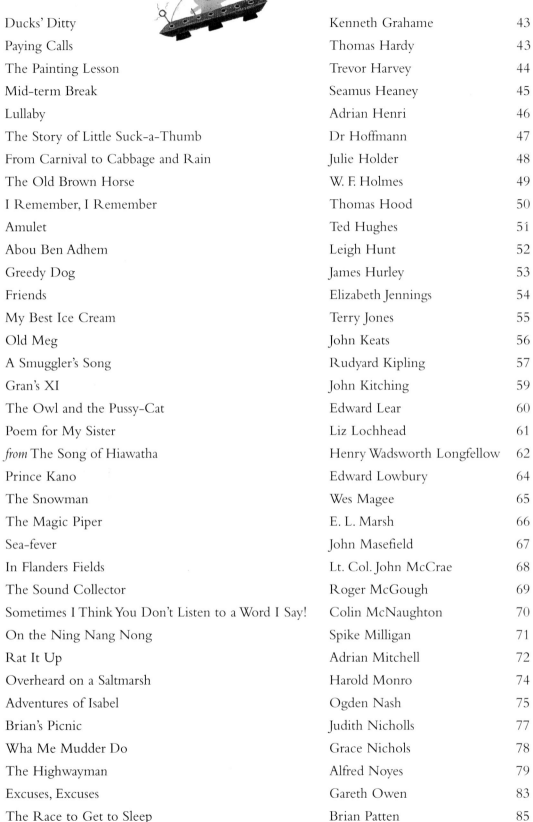

THE HERO OF THE MATCH

hen the Rovers played United in the final yesterday
The factories stopped working and declared a holiday.
On foot, in cars and buses, folk came from miles around
To see the two unbeaten teams meet on the valley ground.

The winter sun was shining and a chill was in the air;
A bitter wind was blowing but no one seemed to care.
They sang and laughed and whistled, and oh but it was grand
To hear the mighty cheer they gave as the players left the stand.

United were the bigger team, they played in black and white;
They were fearsome in the tackle and they dearly loved a fight.
Their defence was firm and steady, their attack knew how to shoot,
And their centre-forward, Banger, was a nasty vicious brute.

The Rovers were a smaller lot, they played in gold and blue;
Their movements were delightful, their passes straight and true.
They could trap and shoot and dribble and they really knew the game.
Their captain was the goalkeeper – Bill Sprightly was his name.

The referee blew his whistle and the tussle had begun.
United's burly winger made a fast and dangerous run,
But the Rover's full-back tackled him as quickly as he could
And kicked the ball out swiftly to where his forwards stood.

Then back and forth the struggle raged and neither side could gain
For United had the strength and force but Rovers had the brain.
At every shot and corner the clubs' supporters roared,
But when the half-time whistle went – neither side had scored!

When the second half had started the Rovers had the ball;
Jim the half-back took it and passed it on to Paul.
He beat the United's full-back, swerved, and gave a shout
As he kicked it past the goalie, who was slow in coming out.

A goal! The crowd was roaring and United gave a groan
But Banger set his teeth and swore he'd win the match alone.
When the centre had been taken he started the attack
And charged a Rovers' forward in the middle of the back.

For half an hour United fired shots into the goal
But Sprightly was unbeatable – he saved them one and all.
Then Banger rushed in madly. He charged with all his might,
And when they picked Bill Sprightly up his face was very white.

His left arm hung down limply, his face was streaked with blood;
His hands and knees were painful where he'd fallen in the mud.
But he pushed the helpers from him and stood, all stiff and sore,
In the goalmouth, undefeated, to keep them out once more.

Five minutes to the whistle! The minutes seemed like hours!
Five minutes to the whistle and then the cup is ours!
So the Rovers hung on grimly, United had no chance
Till there came a sudden opening – Banger saw it at a glance,

Seized the ball and beat the tackle, sent a shot in very low,
But Bill Sprightly had it covered, though his movements were so slow;
Fell, and tipped it round the corner with the hand that he had bent,
Saved a certain equaliser as the final whistle went!

The cheers rang through the valley as the players gathered round
And put Bill on their shoulders as they took him from the ground.
It was only two hours later, when the local doctor spoke,
They knew that Bill's last save was made with an
ELBOW THAT WAS BROKE!

NEIL ADAMS

WHAT TURKEY DOING?

osquito one
mosquito two
mosquito jump
in de old man shoe

Cockroach three
cockroach four
cockroach dance thru
a crack in de floor

Spider five
spider six
spider weaving
a web of tricks

Monkey seven
monkey eight
monkey playing with
pencil and slate

Turkey nine
turkey ten
what turkey doing
in chicken pen?

JOHN AGARD

PLEASE MRS BUTLER

lease Mrs Butler
This boy Derek Drew
Keeps copying my work, Miss.
What shall I do?

Go and sit in the hall, dear.
Go and sit in the sink.
Take your books on the roof, my lamb.
Do whatever you think.

Please Mrs Butler
This boy Derek Drew
Keeps taking my rubber, Miss.
What shall I do?

Keep it in your hand, dear.
Hide it up your vest.
Swallow it if you like, my love.
Do what you think best.

Please Mrs Butler
This boy Derek Drew
Keeps calling me rude names, Miss.
What shall I do?

Lock yourself in the cupboard, dear.
Run away to sea.
Do whatever you can, my flower.
But *don't ask me!*

ALLAN AHLBERG

THE FAIRIES

p the airy mountain,
    Down the rushy glen,
We daren't go a-hunting
    For fear of little men;
Wee folk, good folk,
    Trooping all together;
Green jacket, red cap,
    And white owl's feather!

Down along the rocky shore
    Some make their home;
They live on crispy pancakes
    Of yellow tide-foam;
Some in the reeds
    Of the black mountain lake,
With frogs for their watch-dogs,
    All night awake.

High on the hill-top
    The old King sits;
He is now so old and grey
    He's nigh lost his wits.
With a bridge of white mist
    Columbkill he crosses,
On his stately journeys
    From Slieveleague to Rosses;
Or going up with music
    On cold starry nights,
To sup with the Queen
    Of the gay Northern Lights.

They stole little Bridget
   For seven years long;
When she came down again,
   Her friends were all gone.
They took her lightly back,
   Between the night and morrow,
They thought that she was fast asleep,
   But she was dead with sorrow.
They have kept her ever since
   Deep within the lake,
On a bed of flag-leaves,
   Watching till she wake.

By the craggy hill-side,
   Through the mosses bare,
They have planted thorn-trees
   For pleasure here and there.
Is any man so daring
   As dig them up in spite,
He shall find the thornies set
   In his bed at night.

Up the airy mountain,
   Down the rushy glen,
We daren't go a-hunting
   For fear of little men;
Wee folk, good folk,
   Trooping all together;
Green jacket, red cap,
   And white owl's feather!

WILLIAM ALLINGHAM

NOVEMBER NIGHT COUNTDOWN

 en fat sausages
    sizzling in the fire.
Nine fiery flames
    reaching ever higher.

Eight jumping jacks
    leaping on the ground.
Seven silver sparklers
    whirling round and round.

Six golden fountains
    fizzing in the dark.
Five red rockets
    whizzing across the park.

Four bright Catherine wheels
    spinning on the gate.
Three wide-eyed children
    allowed out very late.

Two proud parents
    watching all the games.
One lonely Guy
    roasting in the flames.

MOIRA ANDREW

DOVER BEACH

he sea is calm to-night.
The tide is full, the moon lies fair
Upon the straits; – on the French coast the light
Gleams and is gone; the cliffs of England stand,
Glimmering and vast, out in the tranquil bay.
Come to the window, sweet is the night-air!
Only, from the long line of spray
Where the sea meets the moon-blanch'd land,
Listen! you hear the grating roar
Of pebbles which the waves draw back, and fling,
At their return, up the high strand,
Begin, and cease, and then again begin,
With tremulous cadence slow, and bring
The eternal note of sadness in.

Sophocles long ago
Heard it on the Ægæan, and it brought
Into his mind the turbid ebb and flow
Of human misery; we
Find also in the sound a thought,
Hearing it by this distant northern sea.
The sea of faith
Was once, too, at the full, and round earth's shore
Lay like the folds of a bright girdle furl'd.
But now I only hear
Its melancholy, long, withdrawing roar,
Retreating to the breath
Of the night-wind down the vast edges drear
And naked shingles of the world.

Ah, love, let us be true
To one another! for the world, which seems
To lie before us like a land of dreams,
So various, so beautiful, so new,
Hath really neither joy, nor love, nor light,
Nor certitude, nor peace, nor help for pain;
And we are here as on a darkling plain
Swept with confused alarms of struggle and flight,
Where ignorant armies clash by night.

MATTHEW ARNOLD

SONG OF THE WORMS

 e have been underground too long,
we have done our work,
we are many and one,
we remember when we were human.

We have lived among roots and stones,
we have sung but no one has listened,
we come into the open air
at night only to love

which disgusts the soles of boots,
their leather strict religion.
We know what a boot looks like
when seen from underneath,
we know the philosophy of boots,
their metaphysic of kicks and ladders.
We are afraid of boots
but contemptuous of the foot that needs them.

Soon we will invade like weeds,
everywhere but slowly:
the captive plants will rebel
with us, fences will topple,
brick walls ripple and fall,

there will be no more boots.
Meanwhile we eat dirt
and sleep; we are waiting
under your feet.
                            When we say Attack
you will hear nothing
at first.

MARGARET ATWOOD

THE DOLLY ON THE DUSTCART

'm the dolly on the dustcart,
I can see you're not impressed,
I'm fixed above the driver's cab,
With wire across me chest,
The dustman see, he spotted me,
Going in the grinder,
And he fixed me on the lorry,
I dunno if that was kinder.

This used to be a lovely dress,
In pink and pretty shades,
But it's torn now, being on the cart,
And black as the ace of spades,
There's dirt all round me face,
And all across me rosy cheeks,
Well, I've had me head thrown back,
But we ain't had no rain for weeks.

I used to be a 'Mama' doll,
Tipped forward, I'd say 'Mum'
But the rain got in me squeaker,
And now I been struck dumb,
I had two lovely blue eyes,
But out in the wind and weather,
One's sunk back in me head like,
And one's gone altogether.

I'm not a soft, flesh coloured dolly,
Modern children like so much,
I'm one of those hard old dollies,
What are very cold to touch,
Modern dolly's underwear,
Leaves me a bit nonplussed,
I haven't got a bra,
But then I haven't got a bust!

Yet I was happy in that dolls house,
I was happy as a Queen,
I never knew that Tiny Tears,
Was coming on the scene,
I heard of dolls with hair that grew,
And I was quite enthralled,
Until I realised *my* head
Was hard and pink . . . and bald.

So I travels with the rubbish,
Out of fashion, out of style,
Out of me environment,
For mile after mile,
No longer prized . . . dustbinized!
Unfeminine, Untidy,
I'm the dolly on the dustcart.
There'll be no collection Friday.

PAM AYRES

MATILDA

Who told Lies, and was Burned to Death

atilda told such Dreadful Lies,
It made one Gasp and Stretch one's Eyes;
Her Aunt, who, from her Earliest Youth,
Had kept a Strict Regard for Truth,
Attempted to Believe Matilda:
The effort very nearly killed her,
And would have done so, had not She
Discovered this Infirmity.
For once, towards the Close of Day,
Matilda, growing tired of play,
And finding she was left alone,
Went tiptoe to the Telephone
And summoned the Immediate Aid
Of London's Noble Fire-Brigade.
Within an hour the Gallant Band
Were pouring in on every hand,
From Putney, Hackney Downs, and Bow,
With Courage high and Hearts a-glow
They galloped, roaring through the Town,
'Matilda's House is Burning Down!'
Inspired by British Cheers and Loud
Proceeding from the Frenzied Crowd,
They ran their ladders through a score
Of windows on the Ball Room Floor;
And took Peculiar Pains to Souse
The Pictures up and down the House,

Until Matilda's Aunt succeeded
In showing them they were not needed,
And even then she had to pay
To get the Men to go away!

It happened that a few Weeks later
Her Aunt was off to the Theatre
To see that Interesting Play
The Second Mrs Tanqueray.
She had refused to take her Niece
To hear this Entertaining Piece:
A deprivation Just and Wise
To Punish her for Telling Lies.
That Night a Fire *did* break out –
You should have heard Matilda Shout!
You should have heard her Scream and Bawl,
And throw the window up and call
To People passing in the Street –
(The rapidly increasing Heat
Encouraging her to obtain
Their confidence) – but all in vain!
For every time She shouted 'Fire!'
They only answered 'Little Liar!'
And therefore when her Aunt returned,
Matilda, and the House, were Burned.

HILAIRE BELLOC

16

THE TIGER

*T*iger! Tiger! burning bright
In the forests of the night,
What immortal hand or eye
Could frame thy fearful symmetry?

In what distant deeps or skies
Burnt the fire of thine eyes?
On what wings dare he aspire?
What the hand dare seize the fire?

And what shoulder, and what art
Could twist the sinews of thy heart?
And, when thy heart began to beat,
What dread hand? and what dread feet?

What the hammer? what the chain?
In what furnace was thy brain?
What the anvil? what dread grasp
Dare its deadly terrors clasp?

When the stars threw down their spears,
And water'd heaven with their tears,
Did he smile his work to see?
Did he who made the lamb make thee?

Tiger! Tiger! burning bright
In the forests of the night,
What immortal hand or eye
Dare frame thy fearful symmetry?

WILLIAM BLAKE

STARTER

i!
I'm cousin Art,
And I like to start
A new thing every day.
But I never finish anything;
At least that's what . . .
they . . .

TONY BRADMAN

from THE PIED PIPER
OF HAMELIN

nto the street the Piper stept,
Smiling first a little smile,
As if he knew what magic slept
In his quiet pipe the while;
Then, like a musical adept,
To blow the pipe his lips he wrinkled,
And green and blue his sharp eyes twinkled
Like a candle-flame where salt is sprinkled;
And ere three shrill notes the pipe uttered,
You heard as if an army muttered;
And the muttering grew to a grumbling;
And the grumbling grew to a mighty
    rumbling;
And out of the houses the rats came
    tumbling.
Great rats, small rats, lean rats, brawny rats,
Brown rats, black rats, grey rats, tawny rats,
Grave old plodders, gay young friskers,
Fathers, mothers, uncles, cousins,
Cocking tails and pricking whiskers,
Families by tens and dozens,
Brothers, sisters, husbands, wives –
Followed the Piper for their lives.
From street to street he piped advancing,
And step for step they followed dancing,
Until they came to the river Weser
Wherein all plunged and perished!

ROBERT BROWNING

NOVEMBER EVENING

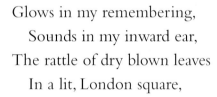ow in November evenings,
 When thick dark falls,
Filling our lanes, and turning
 All mortals into moles,

No moon or stars, no glimmer
 Of lamp, nor means to tell
Hedge from house or haystack
 But by feel and smell,

Glows in my remembering,
 Sounds in my inward ear,
The rattle of dry blown leaves
 In a lit, London square,

And the dim gleam of lamplight
 On leaf-discarding trees
Mingles with urban magic
 These rural secrecies.

GERALD BULLETT

JABBERWOCKY

T was brillig, and the slithy toves
  Did gyre and gimble in the wabe;
All mimsy were the borogroves,
  And the mome raths outgrabe.

'Beware the Jabberwock, my son!
  The jaws that bite, the claws that catch!
Beware the Jubjub bird, and shun
  The frumious Bandersnatch!'

He took his vorpal sword in hand:
  Long time the manxome foe he sought –
So rested he by the Tumtum tree,
  And stood a while in thought.

And as in uffish thought he stood,
  The Jabberwock, with eyes of flame,
Came whiffling through the tulgey wood,
  And burbled as it came!

One, two! One, two! And through and through
  The vorpal blade went snicker-snack!
He left it dead, and with its head
  He went galumphing back.

'And hast thou slain the Jabberwock?
  Come to my arms, my beamish boy!
O frabjous day! Callooh! Callay!'
  He chortled in his joy.

'Twas brillig, and the slithy toves
  Did gyre and gimble in the wabe;
All mimsy were the borogroves,
  And the mome raths outgrabe.

LEWIS CARROLL

COLONEL FAZACKERLEY

Colonel Fazackerley Butterworth-Toast
Bought an old castle complete with a ghost,
But someone or other forgot to declare
To Colonel Fazack that the spectre was there.

On the very first evening, while waiting to dine,
The Colonel was taking a fine sherry wine,
When the ghost, with a furious flash and a flare,
Shot out of the chimney and shivered, 'Beware!'

Colonel Fazackerley put down his glass
And said, 'My dear fellow, that's really first class!
I just can't conceive how you do it at all.
I imagine you're going to a Fancy Dress Ball?'

At this, the dread ghost gave a withering cry.
Said the Colonel (his monocle firm in his eye),
'Now just how you do it I wish I could think.
Do sit down and tell me, and please have a drink.'

The ghost in his phosphorous cloak gave a roar
And floated about between ceiling and floor.
He walked through a wall and returned through a pane
And backed up the chimney and came down again.

Said the Colonel, 'With laughter I'm feeling quite weak!'
(As trickles of merriment ran down his cheek).
'My house-warming party I hope you won't spurn.
You *must* say you'll come and you'll give us a turn!'

CHARLES CAUSLEY

HALLOWE'EN

This is the night when witches fly
On their whizzing broomsticks through the wintry sky;
Steering up the pathway where the stars are strewn,
They stretch skinny fingers to the waking moon.

This is the night when old wives tell
Strange and creepy stories, tales of charm and spell;
Peering at the pictures flaming in the fire
They wait for whispers from a ghostly choir.

This is the night when angels go
In and out the houses, winging o'er the snow;
Clearing out the demons from the countryside
They make it new and ready for Christmastide.

LEONARD CLARK

I THINK MY TEACHER IS A COWBOY

t's not just
That she rides to school on a horse
And carries a Colt 45 in her handbag.

It's not just
the way she walks;
hands hanging over her hips.

It's not just
the way she dresses;
stetson hat and spurs on her boots.

It's not just the way she talks;
calling the playground the corral,
    the Head's room the Sheriff's office,
    the school canteen the chuck wagon,
    the school bus the stagecoach,
    the bike sheds the livery stable.

What gives her away
Is when the hometime pips go.
She slaps her thigh
And cries
'Yee ha!'

JOHN COLDWELL

from THE RIME OF THE ANCIENT MARINER

nd now there came both mist and snow,
And it grew wondrous cold:
And ice, mast-high, came floating by,
As green as emerald.

And through the drifts the snowy clifts
Did send a dismal sheen:
Nor shapes of men nor beasts we ken –
The ice was all between.

The ice was here, the ice was there,
The ice was all around:
It cracked and growled, and roared and howled,
Like noises in a swound!

At length did cross an Albatross,
Thorough the fog it came;
As if it had been a Christian soul,
We hailed it in God's name.

It ate the food it ne'er had eat,
And round and round it flew.
The ice did split with a thunder-fit;
The helmsman steered us through!

And a good south wind sprung up behind;
The Albatross did follow,
And every day, for food or play,
Came to the mariner's hollo!

In mist or cloud, on mast or shroud,
It perched for vespers nine;
Whiles all the night, through fog-smoke white,
Glimmered the white Moon-shine.

'God save thee, ancient Mariner!
From the fiends, that plague thee thus! –
Why look'st thou so?'–'With my cross-bow
I shot the ALBATROSS.'

SAMUEL TAYLOR COLERIDGE

KENNETH

who was too fond of bubble-gum and met an untimely end

The chief defect of Kenneth Plumb
Was chewing too much bubble-gum.
He chewed away with all his might,
Morning, evening, noon and night.
Even (oh, it makes you weep)
Blowing bubbles in his sleep.
He simply couldn't get enough!
His face was covered with the stuff.
As for his teeth – oh, what a sight!
It was a wonder he could bite.
His loving mother and his dad
Both remonstrated with the lad.
Ken repaid them for the trouble
By blowing yet another bubble.

Twas no joke. It isn't funny
Spending all your pocket money
On the day's supply of gum –
Sometimes Kenny felt quite glum.
As he grew, so did his need –
There seemed no limit to his greed:
At ten he often put away
Ninety seven packs a day.

Then at last he went too far –
Sitting in his father's car,

Stuffing gum without a pause,
Found that he had jammed his jaws.
He nudged his dad and pointed to
The mouthful that he couldn't chew.
'Well, spit it out if you can't chew it!'
Ken shook his head. He couldn't do it.
Before long he began to groan –
The gum was solid as a stone.
Dad took him to a builder's yard;
They couldn't help. It was too hard.
They called a doctor and he said,
'This silly boy will soon be dead.
His mouth's so full of bubble-gum
No nourishment can reach his tum.'

Remember Ken and please do not
Go buying too much you-know-what.

WENDY COPE

LITTLE RED RIDING HOOD AND THE WOLF

As soon as Wolf began to feel
That he would like a decent meal,
He went and knocked on Grandma's door.
When Grandma opened it, she saw
The sharp white teeth, the horrid grin,
And Wolfie said, 'May I come in?'
Poor Grandmamma was terrified,
'He's going to eat me up!' she cried.
And she was absolutely right.
He ate her up in one big bite.
But Grandmamma was small and tough,
And Wolfie wailed, 'That's not enough!
I haven't yet begun to feel
That I have had a decent meal!'
He ran around the kitchen yelping,
'I've *got* to have another helping!'
Then added with a frightful leer,
'I'm therefore going to wait right here
Till Little Miss Red Riding Hood
Comes home from walking in the wood.'
He quickly put on Grandma's clothes,
(Of course he hadn't eaten those.)
He dressed himself in coat and hat.
He put on shoes and after that
He even brushed and curled his hair,
Then sat himself in Grandma's chair.
In came the little girl in red.
She stopped. She stared. And then she said,

'What great big ears you have, Grandma.'
'All the better to hear you with,' the Wolf replied.

'*What great big eyes you have, Grandma,*' said Little Red Riding Hood.
'*All the better to see you with,*' the Wolf replied.

He sat there watching her and smiled.
He thought, I'm going to eat this child.
Compared with her old Grandmamma
She's going to taste like caviare.

Then Little Red Riding Hood said, '*But Grandma,*
what a lovely great big furry coat you have on.'
'That's wrong!' cried Wolf. 'Have you forgot
To tell me what BIG TEETH I've got?
Ah well, no matter what you say,
I'm going to eat you anyway.'
The small girl smiles. One eyelid flickers.
She whips a pistol from her knickers.
She aims it at the creature's head
And *bang bang bang*, she shoots him dead.
A few weeks later, in the wood,
I came across Miss Riding Hood.
But what a change! No cloak of red,
No silly hood upon her head.
She said, 'Hello, and do please note
My lovely furry WOLFSKIN COAT.'

ROALD DAHL

THE LISTENERS

'I s there anybody there?' said the Traveller,
Knocking on the moonlit door;
And his horse in the silence champed the grasses
Of the forest's ferny floor:
And a bird flew up out of the turret,
Above the Traveller's head:
And he smote upon the door again a second time;
'Is there anybody there?' he said.
But no one descended to the Traveller;
No head from the leaf-fringed sill
Leaned over and looked into his grey eyes,
Where he stood perplexed and still.
But only a host of phantom listeners
That dwelt in the lone house then
Stood listening in the quiet of the moonlight
To that voice from the world of men:
Stood thronging the faint moonbeams on the dark stair,
That goes down to the empty hall,
Hearkening in an air stirred and shaken
By the lonely Traveller's call.
And he felt in his heart their strangeness,
Their stillness answering his cry,
While his horse moved, cropping the dark turf,
'Neath the starred and leafy sky;
For he suddenly smote on the door, even
Louder, and lifted his head:–
'Tell them I came, and no one answered,
That I kept my word,' he said.
Never the least stir made the listeners,
Though every word he spake
Fell echoing through the shadowiness of the still house

From the one man left awake:
Ay, they heard his foot upon the stirrup,
    And the sound of iron on stone,
And how the silence surged softly backward,
    When the plunging hoofs were gone.

WALTER DE LA MARE

A SLASH OF BLUE

 slash of Blue –
A sweep of Gray –
Some scarlet patches on the way,
Compose an Evening Sky –
A little purple – slipped between
Some Ruby Trousers hurried on –
A Wave of Gold –
A Bank of Day –
This just makes out the Morning Sky.

EMILY DICKINSON

PLEASE SIR!!

There's a fight – Sir!!
In the cloakrooms . . . Sir!!
And Arnie's strangled Paul.
Smithy's strangled Watson
'Cos Watson took his ball.
Barney's ripped his shirt . . . Sir,
And Baker sput on Sue.
She was only tryin' to stop them
And she's got it on her shoe . . .
The helper lady went . . . Sir,
She said she couldn't stay.
Jane's crying in the toilets
And the gerbil's got away. . .

Garnett knocked the cage . . . Sir,
The door, it just flipped back,
And it ran behind the cupboard
And it's stuck inside a crack.
We poked it with a stick . . . Sir,
But the powder paint got spilt.
It's over all the carpet
And it's over Helen's kilt.
I think you ought to come . . . Sir,
Mildred Miles was sick
And all the boys are yellin'
And Martin threw a brick.
It nearly hit John Baily.
And he's goin' to tell his mum,
So shall I say you're comin'
And shall I fetch his mum?
Shall we get the cleaners?

And can I mop the paint?
The new boy's torn his jacket
And he thinks he's going to faint . . .
The other teachers said . . . Sir,
That I should come to you
'Cos you're the Duty Teacher
So you'll know what to do Sir.

PETER DIXON

THE BIRD'S NEST

 I know a place, in the ivy on a tree,
Where a bird's nest is, and the eggs are three,
And the bird is brown, and the eggs are blue,
And the twigs are old, but the moss is new,
And I go quite near, though I think I should have heard
The sound of me watching, if I had been a bird.

JOHN DRINKWATER

THE LION AND ALBERT

here's a famous seaside place called Blackpool,
    That's noted for fresh air and fun,
And Mr and Mrs Ramsbottom
    Went there with young Albert, their son.

A grand little lad was young Albert,
    All dressed in his best; quite a swell
With a stick with an 'orse's 'ead 'andle,
    The finest that Woolworth's could sell.

They didn't think much to the Ocean:
    The waves, they was fiddlin' and small,
There was no wrecks and nobody drownded,
    Fact, nothing to laugh at at all.

So, seeking for further amusement,
    They paid and went into the Zoo,
Where they'd Lions and Tigers and Camels,
    And old ale and sandwiches too.

There were one great big Lion called Wallace;
    His nose were all covered with scars –
He lay in a somnolent posture
    With the side of his face on the bars.

Now Albert had heard about Lions,
    How they was ferocious and wild –
To see Wallace lying so peaceful,
    Well, it didn't seem right to the child.

So straightway the brave little feller,
    Not showing a morsel of fear,
Took his stick with its 'orse's 'ead 'andle
    And poked it in Wallace's ear.

You could see that the Lion didn't like it,
    For giving a kind of a roll,
He pulled Albert inside the cage with 'im,
    And swallowed the little lad 'ole.

Then Pa, who had seen the occurrence,
    And didn't know what to do next,
Said 'Mother! Yon Lion's 'et Albert,'
    And Mother said 'Well, I am vexed!'

Then Mr and Mrs Ramsbottom –
    Quite rightly, when all's said and done –
Complained to the Animal Keeper
    That the Lion had eaten their son.

The keeper was quite nice about it;
    He said 'What a nasty mishap.
Are you sure that it's *your* boy he's eaten?'
    Pa said 'Am I sure? There's his cap!'

The manager had to be sent for.
    He came and he said 'What's to do?'
Pa said 'Yon Lion's 'et Albert,
    And 'im in his Sunday clothes, too.'

Then Mother said 'Right's right, young feller;
   I think it's a shame and a sin
For a Lion to go and eat Albert,
   And after we've paid to come in.'

The manager wanted no trouble,
   He took out his purse right away,
Saying 'How much to settle the matter?'
   And Pa said 'What do you usually pay?'

But Mother had turned a bit awkward
   When she thought where her Albert had gone.
She said 'No! someone's got to be summonsed' –
   So that was decided upon.

Then off they went to the P'lice Station,
   In front of the Magistrate chap;
They told 'im what happened to Albert,
   And proved it by showing his cap.

The Magistrate gave his opinion
   That no one was really to blame
And he said that he hoped the Ramsbottoms
   Would have further sons to their name.

At that Mother got proper blazing,
   'And thank you, sir, kindly,' said she.
'What, waste all our lives raising children
   To feed ruddy Lions? Not me!'

MARRIOTT EDGAR

THE WORD PARTY

 oving words clutch crimson roses,
Rude words sniff and pick their noses,
Sly words come dressed up as foxes,
Short words stand on cardboard boxes,
Common words tell jokes and gabble,
Complicated words play Scrabble,
Swear words stamp around and shout,
Hard words stare each other out,
Foreign words look lost and shrug,
Careless words trip on the rug,
Long words slouch with stooping shoulders,
Code words carry secret folders,
Silly words flick rubber bands,
Hyphenated words hold hands,
Strong words show off, bending metal,
Sweet words call each other 'petal',
Small words yawn and suck their thumbs,
Till at last the morning comes,
Kind words give out farewell posies . . .
Snap! The dictionary closes.

RICHARD EDWARDS

MACAVITY: THE MYSTERY CAT

acavity's a Mystery Cat: he's called the Hidden Paw –
For he's the master criminal who can defy the Law.
He's the bafflement of Scotland Yard, the Flying Squad's despair:
For when they reach the scene of crime – *Macavity's not there*!

Macavity, Macavity, there's no one like Macavity,
He's broken every human law, he breaks the law of gravity.
His powers of levitation would make a fakir stare,
And when you reach the scene of crime – *Macavity's not there*!
You may seek him in the basement, you may look up in the air –
But I tell you once and once again, *Macavity's not there*!

Macavity's a ginger cat, he's very tall and thin;
You would know him if you saw him, for his eyes are sunken in.
His brow is deeply lined with thought, his head is highly domed;
His coat is dusty from neglect, his whiskers are uncombed.
He sways his head from side to side, with movements like a snake;
And when you think he's half asleep, he's always wide awake.

Macavity, Macavity, there's no one like Macavity,
For he's a fiend in feline shape, a monster of depravity.
You may meet him in a by-street, you may see him in the square –
But when a crime's discovered, then *Macavity's not there*!

He's outwardly respectable. (They say he cheats at cards.)
And his footprints are not found in any file of Scotland Yard's.
And when the larder's looted, or the jewel-case is rifled,
Or when the milk is missing, or another Peke's been stifled,
Or the greenhouse glass is broken, and the trellis past repair –
Ay, there's the wonder of the thing! *Macavity's not there*!

And when the Foreign Office find a Treaty's gone astray,
Or the Admiralty lose some plans and drawings by the way,
There may be a scrap of paper in the hall or on the stair –
But it's useless to investigate – *Macavity's not there*!
And when the loss has been disclosed, the Secret Service say:
'It *must* have been Macavity!' – but he's a mile away.
You'll be sure to find him resting, or a-licking of his thumbs,
Or engaged in doing complicated long division sums.

Macavity, Macavity, there's no one like Macavity,
There never was a Cat of such deceitfulness and suavity.
He always has an alibi, and one or two to spare:
At whatever time the deed took place – MACAVITY WASN'T
   THERE!
And they say that all the Cats whose wicked deeds are widely
   known
(I might mention Mungojerrie, I might mention Griddlebone)
Are nothing more than agents for the Cat who all the time
Just controls their operations: the Napoleon of Crime!

T. S. ELIOT

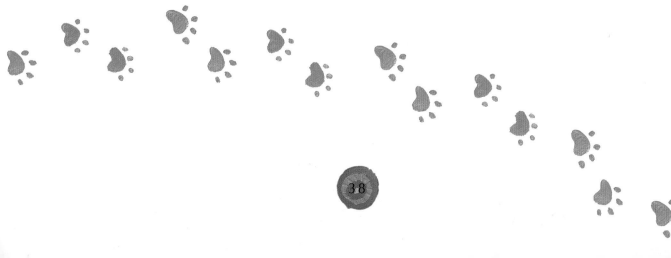

WATER VOLES AND MOLES

ater Voles
Are quite different from Moles.
They have different roles.
They live on river banks in holes,
They can swim like soles.

A Mole, in water, cannot manoeuvre.
He's more like a subterranean Hoover,
A kind of underground earth-mover.

GAVIN EWART

CATS

Cats sleep
Anywhere,
Any table,
Any chair,
Top of piano,
Window-ledge,
In the middle,
On the edge,
Open drawer,
Empty shoe,
Anybody's
Lap will do,
Fitted in a
Cardboard box,
In the cupboard
With your frocks –
Anywhere!
They don't care!
Cats sleep
Anywhere.

ELEANOR FARJEON

THE TREE IN SEASON

pring
The tree hums quietly to itself
a lullaby to the buds
bursting with baby leaves
its branches ride the winds
and in all its new green glory
the tree begins to sing

Summer
The tree stretches in the sun
it knows the birds that fly
the beasts that run, climb and jump
from its heavy loaded branches
it yawns and digs its roots
deep into the still centre
of the spinning earth

Autumn
The tree shivers in the shortening day
its leaves turn gold
the clouds pass
the seeds fall
the tree drops its coins of gold
and the days are rich
with the spending of leaves

Winter
Old branches ache
the tree stands naked in the storms
frozen bleak and bare
deep underground life lies sleeping
the tree sleeps
and waits for the returning sun
to wake him
from his woody dreams

ROBERT FISHER

FOUR O'CLOCK FRIDAY

our o'clock Friday, I'm home at last.
Time to forget the week that's past.
On Monday, in break they stole my ball
And threw it over the playground wall.
On Tuesday afternoon, in games,
They threw mud at me and called me names.
On Wednesday, they trampled my books on the floor,
So Miss kept me in because I swore.
On Thursday, they laughed after the test
'Cause my marks were lower than the rest.
Four o'clock Friday, at last I'm free,
For two whole days they can't get at me.

JOHN FOSTER

STOPPING BY WOODS ON A SNOWY EVENING

hose woods these are I think I know.
His house is in the village, though;
He will not see me stopping here
To watch his woods fill up with snow.

My little horse must think it queer
To stop without a farmhouse near
Between the woods and frozen lake
The darkest evening of the year.

He gives his harness bells a shake
To ask if there is some mistake.
The only other sound's the sweep
Of easy wind and downy flake.

The woods are lovely, dark, and deep,
But I have promises to keep,
And miles to go before I sleep,
And miles to go before I sleep.

ROBERT FROST

DUCKS' DITTY

All along the backwater,
Through the rushes tall,
Ducks are a-dabbling,
Up tails all!

Ducks' tails, drakes' tails,
Yellow feet a-quiver,
Yellow bills all out of sight
Busy in the river!

Slushy green undergrowth
Where the roach swim –
Here we keep our larder,
Cool and full and dim.

Everyone for what he likes!
We like to be
Heads down, tails up,
Dabbling free!

High in the blue above
Swifts whirl and call –
We are down a-dabbling,
Up tails all!

KENNETH GRAHAME

PAYING CALLS

went by footpath and by stile
   Beyond where bustle ends,
Strayed here a mile and there a mile
   And called upon some friends.

It was the time of midsummer
   When they had used to roam;
But now, though tempting was the air,
   I found them all at home.

On certain ones I had not seen
   For years past did I call,
And then on others who had been
   The oldest friends of all.

I spoke to one and other of them
   By mound and stone and tree
Of things we had done ere days were dim,
   But they spoke not to me.

THOMAS HARDY

THE PAINTING LESSON

 hat's THAT dear?'
asked the new teacher.

'It's Mummy,' I replied.

'But mums aren't green and orange!
You really haven't TRIED.
You don't just paint in SPLODGES
– You're old enough to know
You need to THINK before you work . . .
Now – have another go.'

She helped me draw two arms and legs,
A face with sickly smile,
A rounded body, dark brown hair,
A hat – and, in a while,
She stood back (with her face bright pink):
'That's SO much better – don't you think?'

But she turned white
At ten to three
When an orange-green blob
Collected me.

'Hi, Mum!'

TREVOR HARVEY

MID-TERM BREAK

I sat all morning in the college sick-bay
Counting bells knelling classes to a close.
At two o'clock our neighbours drove me home.

In the porch I met my father crying –
He had always taken funerals in his stride –
And Big Jim Evans saying it was a hard blow.

The baby cooed and laughed and rocked the pram
When I came in, and I was embarrassed
By old men standing up to shake my hand

And tell me they were 'sorry for my trouble'.
Whispers informed strangers I was the eldest,
Away at school, as my mother held my hand

In hers and coughed out angry tearless sighs.
At ten o'clock the ambulance arrived
With the corpse, stanched and bandaged by the nurses.

Next morning I went up into the room. Snowdrops
And candles soothed the bedside; I saw him
For the first time in six weeks. Paler now,

Wearing a poppy bruise on his left temple,
He lay in the four foot box as in his cot.
No gaudy scars, the bumper knocked him clear.

A four foot box, a foot for every year.

SEAMUS HEANEY

LULLABY

oken and then lulled by the seagulls
Sleep till the sea-fret rolls by
Turn on your pillow till morning
Back to the opening sky

Sleep though the dreams may come crowding
Like mists across the bay
Night-birds will hover above you
Cry to the echoing day

Sleep tho' the aeroplanes lull you
Dull through the evening skies
Sleep with the seabirds for guardians
Distances lost in their eyes

Sandpipers wade in the marshes
Curlews awake on the plain
Turn to the cobblestone sunlight
Wake to the morning again.

ADRIAN HENRI

THE STORY OF LITTLE SUCK-A-THUMB

ne day, Mamma said: 'Conrad dear.
I must go out and leave you here.
But mind now, Conrad, what I say,
Don't suck your thumb while I'm away.
The great tall tailor always comes
To little boys that suck their thumbs,
And ere they dream what he's about,
He takes his great sharp scissors out
And cuts their thumbs clean off, – and then,
You know, they never grow again.'

Mamma had scarcely turn'd her back,
The thumb was in, Alack! Alack!

The door flew open, in he ran,
The great, long, red-legg'd scissor-man.
Oh! children, see! the tailor's come
And caught out little Suck-a-Thumb.
Snip! Snap! Snip! the scissors go;
And Conrad cries out – Oh! Oh! Oh!
Snip! Snap! Snip! They go so fast,
That both his thumbs are off at last.

Mamma comes home; there Conrad stands.
And looks quite sad, and shows his hands, –
'Ah!' said Mamma 'I knew he'd come
To naughty little Suck-a-Thumb.'

DR HOFFMANN

FROM CARNIVAL TO CABBAGE AND RAIN

he narrow streets
Are smiles wide
Carnival has come to town.
Granny has a rose in her teeth
The baby wears a crown.
Everyone has come outside
To follow pied piper bands
Wearing dressing up clothes
Dancing hand in hands.
Hearts and blood
Beat to the drum.
Children free balloons
'I gave mine to the sun'
A child cries.
Strangers are greeted as friends
Under the blue skies.
The streets vibrate
Deep into the night
And rock from end to ends.
Children sleep on parents' shoulders
Late and light
Weaving Carnival into dreams
Round rainbow bends.

They shop for cabbage today
In narrow streets
Polite and grey.
Glitter shines
Down the drain
And people say
'Now it can rain.'

JULIE HOLDER

THE OLD BROWN HORSE

The old brown horse looks over the fence
    In a weary sort of way;
He seems to be saying to all who pass:
    'Well, folks, I've had my day –
I'm simply watching the world go by,
    And nobody seems to mind,
As they're dashing past in their motor-cars,
    A horse who is lame and half-blind.'

The old brown horse has a shaggy coat,
    But once he was young and trim,
And he used to trot through the woods and lanes
    With the man who was fond of him.
But his master rides in a motor-car,
    And it makes him feel quite sad
When he thinks of the days that used to be,
    And of all the times they had.

Sometimes a friendly soul will stop
    Near the fence, where the tired old head
Rests wearily on the topmost bar,
    And a friendly word is said.
Then the old brown horse gives a little sigh
    As he feels the kindly touch
Of a hand on his mane or his shaggy coat,
    And he doesn't mind so much.

So if you pass by the field one day,
    Just stop for a word or two
With the old brown horse who was once as young
    And as full of life as you.
He'll love the touch of your soft young hand,
    And I know he'll seem to say –
'Oh, thank you, friend, for the kindly thought
    For a horse who has had his day.'

W. F. HOLMES

I REMEMBER, I REMEMBER

I remember, I remember,
   The house where I was born,
The little window where the sun
   Came peeping in at morn;
He never came a wink too soon,
   Nor brought too long a day,
But now, I often wish the night
   Had borne my breath away.

I remember, I remember,
   Where I was used to swing;
And thought the air must rush as fresh
   To swallows on the wing:
My spirit flew in feathers then,
   That is so heavy now,
And summer pools could hardly cool
   The fever on my brow!

I remember, I remember,
   The roses, red and white;
The violets, and the lily-cups,
   Those flowers made of light!
The lilacs where the robin built,
   And where my brother set
The laburnum on his birthday –
   The tree is living yet!

I remember, I remember,
   The fir trees dark and high;
I used to think their slender tops
   Were close against the sky:
It was a childish ignorance,
   But now 'tis little joy
To know I'm farther off from Heav'n
   Than when I was a boy.

THOMAS HOOD

AMULET

 nside the wolf's fang, the mountain of heather.
Inside the mountain of heather, the wolf's fur.
Inside the wolf's fur, the ragged forest.
Inside the ragged forest, the wolf's foot.
Inside the wolf's foot, the stony horizon.
Inside the stony horizon, the wolf's tongue.
Inside the wolf's tongue, the doe's tears.
Inside the doe's tears, the frozen swamp.
Inside the frozen swamp, the wolf's blood.
Inside the wolf's blood, the snow wind.
Inside the snow wind, the wolf's eye.
Inside the wolf's eye, the North star.
Inside the North star, the wolf's fang.

TED HUGHES

ABOU BEN ADHEM

bou Ben Adhem (may his tribe increase!)
Awoke one night from a deep dream of peace,
And saw, within the moonlight in his room,
Making it rich, and like a lily in bloom,
An angel writing in a book of gold: –
Exceeding peace had made Ben Adhem bold,
And to the presence in the room he said,
'What writest thou?' – The vision raised its head,
And with a look made of all sweet accord,
Answered, 'The names of those who love the Lord.'
'And is mine one?' said Abou. 'Nay, not so,'
Replied the angel. Abou spoke more low,
But cheerly still; and said, 'I pray thee, then,
Write me as one that loves his fellow men.'

The angel wrote, and vanished. The next night
It came again with a great wakening light,
And showed the names whom love of God had blest,
And lo! Ben Adhem's name led all the rest.

LEIGH HUNT

GREEDY DOG

 This dog will eat anything.

Apple cores and bacon fat,
Milk you poured out for the cat.
He likes the string that ties the roast
And relishes hot buttered toast.
Hide your chocolates! He's a thief,
He'll even eat your handkerchief.
And if you don't like sudden shocks,
Carefully conceal your socks.
Leave some soup without a lid
And you'll wish you never did.
When you think he must be full,
You find him gobbling bits of wool,
Orange peel or paper bags,
Dusters and old cleaning rags.

This dog will eat anything,
Except for mushrooms and cucumber.

Now what is wrong with those, I wonder.

JAMES HURLEY

FRIENDS

I fear it's very wrong of me
And yet I must admit,
When someone offers friendship
I want the *whole* of it.
I don't want everybody else
To share my friends with me.
At least, I want *one* special one,
Who indisputedly,

Likes me much more than all the rest,
Who's always on my side,
Who never cares what others say,
Who lets me come and hide
Within his shadow, in his house –
It doesn't matter where –
Who lets me simply be myself,
Who's always, *always* there.

ELIZABETH JENNINGS

MY BEST ICE CREAM

T he best ice cream
I think I've ever tasted
Was the one I fell in
When I was only ten.
It was huge, I tell you –
The size of a small mountain,
And there is no telling
When we'll see its like again.

The best stick of rock
I think I've ever eaten
Was the one I climbed up
When I was only four.
It took six days,
Then I started eating downwards
And when midnight chimed
I had gnawed it to the floor!

The best fizzy drink
I think I've ever swallowed
Was the one I sailed across
When I was only eight.
It was wide across
As the great Pacific Ocean,
And I drank it with an albatross
Whose name was Kate.

TERRY JONES

OLD MEG

ld Meg she was a Gipsey,
    And liv'd upon the Moors;
Her bed it was the brown heath turf,
    And her house was out of doors.

Her apples were swart blackberries,
    Her currants, pods o'broom;
Her wine was dew of the wild white rose,
    Her book a churchyard tomb.

Her Brothers were the craggy hills,
    Her Sisters larchen trees;
Alone with her great family
    She liv'd as she did please.

No breakfast had she many a morn,
    No dinner many a noon,
And, 'stead of supper, she would stare
    Full hard against the moon.

But every morn, of woodbine fresh
    She made her garlanding,
And, every night, the dark glen Yew
    She wove, and she would sing.

And with her fingers, old and brown,
    She plaited Mats o' Rushes,
And gave them to the cottagers
    She met among the Bushes.

Old Meg was brave as Margaret Queen
    And tall as Amazon;
An old red blanket cloak she wore,
    A chip hat had she on.
God rest her aged bones somewhere!
    She died full long agone!

JOHN KEATS

A SMUGGLER'S SONG

f you wake at midnight, and hear a horse's feet,
Don't go drawing back the blind, or looking in the street.
Them that asks no questions isn't told a lie.
Watch the wall, my darling, while the Gentlemen go by!
   Five and twenty ponies,
   Trotting through the dark –
   Brandy for the Parson,
   'Baccy for the Clerk;
   Laces for a lady, letters for a spy,
And watch the wall, my darling, while the Gentlemen go by!

Running round the woodlump if you chance to find
Little barrels, roped and tarred, all full of brandy-wine,
Don't you shout to come and look, nor use 'em for your play.
Put the brushwood back again – and they'll be gone next day!

If you see a stable-door setting open wide;
If you see a tired horse lying down inside;
If your mother mends a coat cut about and tore;
If the lining's wet and warm – don't you ask no more!

If you meet King George's men, dressed in blue and red,
You be careful what you say, and mindful what is said.
If they call you 'pretty maid', and chuck you 'neath the chin,
Don't you tell where no one is, nor yet where no one's been!

Knocks and footsteps round the house – whistles after dark –
You've no call for running out till the house-dogs bark.
Trusty's here, and *Pincher's* here, and see how dumb they lie –
They don't fret to follow when the Gentlemen go by!

If you do as you've been told, 'likely there's a chance,
You'll be give a dainty doll, all the way from France,
With a cap of Valenciennes, and a velvet hood –
A present from the Gentlemen, along o' being good!
    Five and twenty ponies,
    Trotting through the dark –
    Brandy for the Parson,
    'Baccy for the Clerk.
Them that asks no questions isn't told a lie –
Watch the wall, my darling, while the Gentlemen go by!

RUDYARD KIPLING

GRAN'S XI

My grandma's in a football team.
Her age is seventy-eight.
She's no longer like a palm tree
Standing waiting for a date.

The goalie in my grandma's team,
Her age is seventy-four.
Opponents rarely score a goal.
She's built like a grey barn door.

The striker is a real antique,
Captain at eighty-eight.
She's vicious, mean, and fouls a lot;
The kind of striker goalies hate.

Two of Grandma's football team
Are quite acutely deaf.
They shout and wave most rudely
At every weekend ref.

Most of Grandma's football team
Have aged, aching bones,
But in the showers, after games,
No single player moans.

The other week – a rare defeat.
They lost: three goals to five.
But they don't seem to care a lot.
They're just glad to be alive!

JOHN KITCHING

THE OWL AND THE PUSSY-CAT

*T*he Owl and the Pussy-Cat went to sea
   In a beautiful pea-green boat:
They took some honey, and plenty of money
   Wrapped up in a five-pound note.
The Owl looked up to the stars above,
   And sang to a small guitar,
'O lovely Pussy, O Pussy, my love,
   What a beautiful Pussy you are,
      You are,
      You are!
   What a beautiful Pussy you are!'

Pussy said to the Owl, 'You elegant fowl,
   How charmingly sweet you sing!
Oh! let us be married; too long we have tarried
   But what shall we do for a ring?'
They sailed away, for a year and a day,
   To the land where the bong-tree grows;
And there in a wood a Piggy-wig stood,
   With a ring at the end of his nose,
      His nose,
      His nose,
   With a ring at the end of his nose.

'Dear Pig, are you willing to sell for one shilling
   Your ring?' Said the Piggy, 'I will.'
So they took it away, and were married next day
   By the turkey who lives on the hill.
They dined on mince and slices of quince,
   Which they ate with a runcible spoon;
And hand in hand, on the edge of the sand,
   They danced by the light of the moon,
      The moon,
      The moon,
   They danced by the light of the moon.

EDWARD LEAR

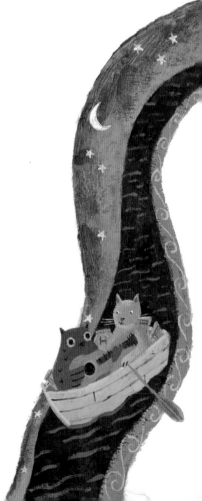

POEM FOR MY SISTER

y little sister likes to try my shoes,
to strut in them,
admire her spindle-thin twelve-year-old legs
in this season's styles.
She says they fit her perfectly,
but wobbles
on their high heels, they're
hard to balance.

I like to watch my little sister
playing hopscotch, admire the neat hops-and-skips of her,
their quick peck,
never missing their mark, not
overstepping the line.
She is competent at peever.

I try to warn my little sister
about unsuitable shoes,
point out my own distorted feet, the calluses,
odd patches of hard skin.
I should not like to see her
in my shoes.
I wish she should stay
sure-footed,
sure-footed, sensibly shod.

LIZ LOCHHEAD

from THE SONG OF HIAWATHA

And erect upon the mountains,
Gitche Manito, the mighty,
Smoked the calumet, the Peace-Pipe,
As a signal to the nations.
    And the smoke rose slowly, slowly,
Through the tranquil air of morning,
First a single line of darkness,
Then a denser, bluer vapor,
Then a snow-white cloud unfolding,
Like the tree-tops of the forest,
Ever rising, rising, rising,
Till it touched the top of heaven,
Till it broke against the heaven,
And rolled outward all around it.
  From the Vale of Tawasentha,
From the Valley of Wyoming,
From the groves of Tuscaloosa,
From the far-off Rocky Mountains,
From the Northern lakes and rivers
All the tribes beheld the signal,
Saw the distant smoke ascending,
The Pukwana of the Peace-Pipe.

And the Prophets of the nations
Said: 'Behold it, the Pukwana!
By the signal of the Peace-Pipe,
Bending like a wand of willow,
Waving like a hand that beckons,
Gitche Manito, the mighty,
Calls the tribes of men together,
Calls the warriors to his council!'

Down the rivers, o'er the prairies,
Came the warriors of the nations,
Came the Delawares and Mohawks,
Came the Choctaws and Camanches,
Came the Shoshonies and Blackfeet,
Came the Pawnees and Omahas,

Came the Mandans and Dacotahs,
Came the Hurons and Ojibways,
All the warriors drawn together
By the signal of the Peace-Pipe,
To the Mountains of the Prairie,
To the great Red Pipe-stone Quarry.

HENRY WADSWORTH LONGFELLOW

PRINCE KANO

I n a dark wood Prince Kano, lost his way
And searched in vain through the long summer's day.
At last, when night was near, he came in sight
Of a small clearing filled with yellow light,
And there, bending beside his brazier, stood
A charcoal burner wearing a black hood.
The Prince cried out for joy: 'Good friend, I'll give
What you will ask: guide me to where I live.'
The man pulled back his hood: he had no face −
Where it should be there was an empty space.
Half dead with fear the Prince staggered away,
Rushed blindly through the wood till break of day;
And then he saw a larger clearing, filled
With houses, people; but his soul was chilled,
He looked around for comfort, and his search
Led him inside a small, half-empty church
Where monks prayed. 'Father,' to one he said,
'I've seen a dreadful thing; I am afraid.'
'What did you see, my son?' 'I saw a man
Whose face was like. . .' and, as the Prince began,
The monk drew back his hood and seemed to hiss
Pointing to where his face should be, 'Like this?'

EDWARD LOWBURY

THE SNOWMAN

Child's play:
stacked snow,
scarf, hat,
carrot nose,
stick and
round pebbles
for eyes.

He freezes:
fat target
for snowballers
who dearly
want to
knock off
his block.

Three days,
and grey
with age
he shrinks
as warmth
turns the
world green.

Scarf, hat
are reclaimed.
Pebbles mark
his grave,
damp lawn
where a
child plays.

WES MAGEE

THE MAGIC PIPER

 here piped a piper in the wood
Strange music – soft and sweet –
And all the little wild things
Came hurrying to his feet.

They sat around him on the grass,
Enchanted, unafraid,
And listened, as with shining eyes
Sweet melodies he made.

The wood grew green, and flowers sprang up,
The birds began to sing;
For the music it was magic,
And the piper's name was – Spring!

E. L. MARSH

SEA-FEVER

 must down to the seas again, to the lonely sea and the sky,
And all I ask is a tall ship and a star to steer her by,
And a wheel's kick and the wind's song and the white sail's shaking,
And a grey mist on the sea's face and a grey dawn breaking.

I must down to the seas again, for the call of the running tide
Is a wild call and a clear call that may not be denied;
And all I ask is a windy day with the white clouds flying,
And the flung spray and the blown spume, and the seagulls crying.

I must down to the seas again, to the vagrant gypsy life,
To the gull's way and the whale's way where the wind's like a
    whetted knife;
And all I ask is a merry yarn from a laughing fellow-rover,
And quiet sleep and a sweet dream when the long trick's over.

JOHN MASEFIELD

IN FLANDERS FIELDS

n Flanders Fields the poppies blow
Between the crosses, row on row,
That mark our place: and in the sky
The larks, still bravely singing, fly
Scarce heard amid the guns below.
We are the dead. Short days ago
We lived, felt dawn, saw sunset glow,
Loved, and were loved, and now we lie
In Flanders Fields.
Take up your quarrel with the foe;
To you from failing hands we throw
The torch; be yours to hold it high.
If ye break faith with us who die
We shall not sleep, though poppies grow
In Flanders Fields.

LT. COL. JOHN MCCRAE

THE SOUND COLLECTOR

 stranger called this morning
Dressed all in black and grey
Put every sound into a bag
And carried them away

The whistling of the kettle
The turning of the lock
The purring of the kitten
The ticking of the clock

The popping of the toaster
The crunching of the flakes
When you spread the marmalade
The scraping noise it makes

The hissing of the frying-pan
The ticking of the grill
The bubbling of the bathtub
As it starts to fill

The drumming of the raindrops
On the window-pane
When you do the washing-up
The gurgle of the drain

The crying of the baby
The squeaking of the chair
The swishing of the curtain
The creaking of the stair

A stranger called this morning
He didn't leave his name
Left us only silence
Life will never be the same.

ROGER MCGOUGH

SOMETIMES I THINK YOU DON'T LISTEN TO A WORD I SAY!

id you have a hard day at the office, dear?

The usual, you know, nothing special, I fear;
I fell in with pirates and lost both my knees,
Came down with ffotherington's foot-rot disease!
Was mugged by an octopus, chased by a pig,
On the bus a banana set fire to my wig.
I met a magician who sawed me in two
And I had to be stuck back together with glue.
I encountered a cow who was over the moon,
The lift-cable snapped and I plunged to my doom.
I was beaten at chess by a chocolate éclair,
I looked in the mirror, but I wasn't there!
Ran off with the circus, became, if you please,
The daring young man on the flying trapeze.
Had words with an alien, barked at a dog,
Married a dinosaur, fell off a log.
I rescued a man who was falling asleep,
Had lunch with a wood louse (a right little creep!),
Was kidnapped at gunpoint by Princess Diana,
Trussed up in a sack and then dumped in Havana;
Escaped without problem: I hijacked a jet,
Flew home to England and guess who I met?
The Princess and Princes Anne, Charles, Andrew, Eddy. . .

That's very nice dear, your dinner is ready

COLIN MCNAUGHTON

ON THE NING NANG NONG

On the Ning Nang Nong
Where the Cows go Bong!
And the Monkeys all say Boo!
There's a Nong Nang Ning
Where the trees go Ping!
And the tea pots Jibber Jabber Joo.
On the Nong Ning Nang
All the mice go Clang!
And you just can't catch 'em when they do!
So it's Ning Nang Nong!
Cows go Bong!
Nong Nang Ning!
Trees go Ping!
Nong Ning Nang!
The mice go Clang!
What a noisy place to belong,
Is the Ning Nang Ning Nang Nong!!

SPIKE MILLIGAN

RAT IT UP

'mon everybody
Slap some grease on those paws
Get some yellow on your teeth
And, uh, sharpen up your claws

There's a whole lot of sausage
We're gonna swallow down
We're gonna jump out the sewers
And rock this town

Cos we're ratting it up
Yes we're ratting it up
Well we're ratting it up
For a ratting good time tonight

Ain't got no compass
You don't need no map
Just follow your snout
Hey, watch out for that trap!

You can take out a poodle
You can beat up a cat
But if you can't lick a ferret
You ain't no kind of rat

Cos we're ratting it up
Yes we're ratting it up
Well we're ratting it up
For a ratting good time tonight

Now you can sneak in the henhouse
Roll out the eggs
But if the farmer comes running
Bite his hairy legs

Check that cheese for poison
Before you eat
Or you'll wind up being served up
As ratburger meat

    Cos we're ratting it up
    Yes we're ratting it up
    Well we're ratting it up
    For a ratting good time tonight

This rat was born to rock
This rat was born to roll
I don't give no monkey's
Bout your pest control

So push off pussy-cat
Push off pup
We're the rocking rodents
And we're ratting it up

    Yeah we're ratting it up
    Yeah we're ratting it up
    Well we're ratting it up
    For a ratting good time tonight!

ADRIAN MITCHELL

OVERHEARD ON A SALTMARSH

ymph, nymph, what are your beads?

Green glass, goblin. Why do you stare at them?

Give them me.

No.

Give them me. Give them me.

No.

Then I will howl all night in the reeds,
Lie in the mud and howl for them.

Goblin, why do you love them so?

They are better than stars or water,
Better than voices of winds that sing,
Better than any man's fair daughter,
Your green glass beads on a silver ring.

Hush, I stole them out of the moon.

Give me your beads, I desire them.

No.

I will howl in a deep lagoon
For your green glass beads, I love them so,
Give them me. Give them.

No.

HAROLD MONRO

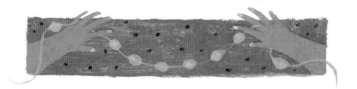

ADVENTURES OF ISABEL

sabel met an enormous bear,
Isabel, Isabel, didn't care;
The bear was hungry, the bear was ravenous,
The bear's big mouth was cruel and cavernous.
The bear said, Isabel, glad to meet you,
How do, Isabel, now I'll eat you!
Isabel, Isabel, didn't worry,
Isabel didn't scream or scurry.
She washed her hands and she straightened her hair up,
Then Isabel quietly ate the bear up.

Once in a night as black as pitch
Isabel met a wicked old witch.
The witch's face was cross and wrinkled,
The witch's gums with teeth were sprinkled.
Ho ho, Isabel! the old witch crowed,
I'll turn you into an ugly toad!
Isabel, Isabel, didn't worry,
Isabel didn't scream or scurry,
She showed no rage and she showed no rancour,
But she turned the witch into milk and drank her.

Isabel met a hideous giant,
Isabel continued self-reliant.
The giant was hairy, the giant was horrid,
He had one eye in the middle of his forehead.
Good morning, Isabel, the giant said,
I'll grind your bones to make my bread.
Isabel, Isabel, didn't worry,
Isabel didn't scream or scurry.
She nibbled the zwieback that she always fed off,
And when it was gone, she cut the giant's head off.

Isabel met a troublesome doctor,
He punched and he poked till he really shocked her.
The doctor's talk was of coughs and chills
And the doctor's satchel bulged with pills.
The doctor said unto Isabel,
Swallow this, it will make you well.
Isabel, Isabel, didn't worry,
Isabel didn't scream or scurry.
She took those pills from the pill concocter,
And Isabel calmly cured the doctor.

OGDEN NASH

BRIAN'S PICNIC

W e've . . .

   cheese rolls, chicken rolls,
   beef rolls, ham;
   choose now, quickly, Brian –
   bacon, beans or Spam?

   I WANT A DOUGHNUT!

We've . . .

   egg and cress and sausages,
   good old lettuce leaf;
   come on, Brian, take some now –
   there's turkey, tuna, beef . . .

   I WANT A DOUGHNUT!

We've . . .

   treacle tart and apple tart,
   biscuits, blackberries, cake –
   Take which one you feel like,
   Brian, come along now, take!

   I WANT A DOUGHNUT!

There's . . .

   jelly next or trifle,
   everything must go!
   Quickly, Brian, pass your plate –
   is it yes or no?

   I WANT A DOUGHNUT!

LAST CHANCE!

We've . . .

   sponge cake, fruit cake,
   eat it *any* way!
   Peanut butter, best rump steak . . .
   what is that you say?

   I WANT A DOUGHNUT!

JUDITH NICHOLLS

WHA ME MUDDER DO

ek me tell you wha me Mudder do
wha me mudder do
wha me mudder do

Me mudder pound plantain mek fufu
Me mudder catch crab mek calaloo stew

Mek me tell you wha me mudder do
wha me mudder do
wha me mudder do

Me mudder beat hammer
Me mudder turn screw
she paint chair red
then she paint it blue

Mek me tell you wha me mudder do
wha me mudder do
wha me mudder do

Me mudder chase bad-cow
with one 'Shoo'
she paddle down river
in she own canoe
Ain't have nothing
dat me mudder can't do
Ain't have nothing
dat me mudder can't do

Mek me tell you

GRACE NICHOLS

THE HIGHWAYMAN

Part One

he wind was a torrent of darkness among the gusty trees,
The moon was a ghostly galleon tossed upon cloudy seas,
The road was a ribbon of moonlight over the purple moor,
And the highwayman came riding –
    Riding – riding –
The highwayman came riding, up to the old inn-door.

He'd a French cocked-hat on his forehead, a bunch of lace at his chin,
A coat of the claret velvet, and breeches of brown doeskin:
They fitted with never a wrinkle; his boots were up to the thigh!
And he rode with a jewelled twinkle,
    His pistol butts a-twinkle,
His rapier hilt a-twinkle, under the jewelled sky.

Over the cobbles he clattered and clashed in the dark inn-yard,
And he tapped with his whip on the shutters, but all was locked
    and barred:
He whistled a tune to the window, and who should be waiting there
But the landlord's black-eyed daughter,
    Bess, the landlord's daughter,
Plaiting a dark red love-knot into her long black hair.

And dark in the dark old inn-yard a stable-wicket creaked
Where Tim, the ostler, listened; his face was white and peaked,
His eyes were hollows of madness, his hair like mouldy hay;
But he loved the landlord's daughter,
    The landlord's red-lipped daughter:
Dumb as a dog he listened, and he heard the robber say –

'One kiss, my bonny sweetheart, I'm after a prize tonight,
But I shall be back with the yellow gold before the morning light.
Yet if they press me sharply, and harry me through the day,
Then look for me by moonlight:
Watch for me by moonlight:
I'll come to thee by moonlight, though Hell should bar the way.'

He rose upright in the stirrups, he scarce could reach her hand;
But she loosened her hair i' the casement! His face burnt like a brand
As the black cascade of perfume came tumbling over his breast;
And he kissed its waves in the moonlight,
(Oh, sweet black waves in the moonlight)
Then he tugged at his reins in the moonlight, and galloped away to the West.

Part Two
He did not come in the dawning; he did not come at noon;
And out of the tawny sunset, before the rise o' the moon,
When the road was a gypsy's ribbon, looping the purple moor,
A red-coat troop came marching –
Marching – marching –
King George's men came marching, up to the old inn-door.

They said no word to the landlord, they drank his ale instead;
But they gagged his daughter and bound her to the foot of her narrow bed.
Two of them knelt at her casement, with muskets at the side!
There was death at every window;
And Hell at one dark window;
For Bess could see, through her casement, the road that *he* would ride.

They had tied her up to attention, with many a sniggering jest:
They had bound a musket beside her, with the barrel beneath her breast!
'Now keep good watch!' and they kissed her.
She heard the dead man say –
Look for me by moonlight;
Watch for me by moonlight;

I'll come to thee by moonlight, though Hell should bar the way!

She twisted her hands behind her; but all the knots held good!
She writhed her hands till her fingers were wet with sweat or blood!
They stretched and strained in the darkness, and the hours crawled by like
    years;
Till, now, on the stroke of midnight,
      Cold, on the stroke of midnight,
The tip of one finger touched it! The trigger at least was hers!

The tip of one finger touched it; she strove no more for the rest!
Up, she stood up to attention, with the barrel beneath her breast,
She would not risk their hearing; she would not strive again;
For the road lay bare in the moonlight,
      Blank and bare in the moonlight;
And the blood of her veins in the moonlight throbbed to her Love's refrain.

Tlot-tlot, tlot-tlot! Had they heard it? The horse-hoofs ringing clear –
Tlot-tlot, tlot-tlot, in the distance? Were they deaf that they did not hear?
Down the ribbon of moonlight, over the brow of the hill,
The highwayman came riding,
      Riding, riding!
The red-coats looked to their priming! She stood up straight and still!

Tlot-tlot, in the frosty silence! *Tlot-tlot* in the echoing night!
Nearer he came and nearer! Her face was like a light!
Her eyes grew wide for a moment; she drew one last deep breath,
Then her finger moved in the moonlight,
      Her musket shattered the moonlight,
Shattered her breast in the moonlight and warned him – with her death.

He turned; he spurred him westward; he did not know who stood
Bowed with her head o'er the musket, drenched with her own red blood!
Not till the dawn he heard it, and slowly blanched to hear
How Bess, the landlord's daughter,

The landlord's black-eyed daughter,
Had watched for her Love in the moonlight; and died in the darkness there.

Back, he spurred like a madman, shrieking a curse to the sky,
With the white road smoking behind him, and his rapier brandished high!
Blood-red were his spurs i' the golden noon; wine-red was his velvet coat;
When they shot him down on the highway,
　　Down like a dog on the highway,
And he lay in his blood on the highway, with the bunch of lace at his throat.

And still of a winter's night, they say, when the wind is in the trees,
When the moon is a ghostly galleon tossed upon cloudy seas,
When the road is a ribbon of moonlight over the purple moor,
A highwayman comes riding –
　　Riding – riding –
A highwayman comes riding, up to the old inn-door.

Over the cobbles he clatters and clangs in the dark inn-yard;
And he taps with his whip on the shutters, but all is locked and barred:
He whistles a tune to the window, and who should be waiting there
But the landlord's black-eyed daughter,
　　Bess, the landlord's daughter,
Plaiting a dark red love-knot into her long black hair.

ALFRED NOYES

EXCUSES, EXCUSES

ate again, Blenkinsopp?

What's the excuse this time?

Not my fault, sir.

Whose fault is it then?

Grandma's, sir.

Grandma's? What did she do?

She died, sir.

Died?

She's seriously dead all right, sir.

That makes four grandmothers this term, Blenkinsopp.

And all on P.E. days.

I know. It's very upsetting, sir.

How many grandmothers have you got, Blenkinsopp?

Grandmothers, sir? None, sir.

You said you had four.

All dead, sir.

And what about yesterday, Blenkinsopp?

What about yesterday, sir?

You were absent yesterday.

That was the dentist, sir.

The dentist died?

No, sir. My teeth, sir.

You missed the maths test, Blenkinsopp!

I'd been looking forward to it, sir.

Right, line up for P.E.

Can't, sir.

No such words as 'can't', Blenkinsopp.

No kit, sir.

Where is it?

Home, sir.

What's it doing at home?

Not ironed, sir.

Couldn't you iron it?

Can't, sir.

Why not?

Bad hand, sir.

Who usually does it?

Grandma, sir.

Why couldn't she do it?

Dead, sir.

GARETH OWEN

THE RACE TO GET TO SLEEP

hey're on their marks, they're set,
They're off!

Matthew's kicking off his shoes!
Penny's struggling out of her jumper!
He's ripping off his trousers!
She's got one sock off! Now the other's off!
But Matthew's still winning! No, he's not!
It's Penny! Penny's in the lead!

She's down to her knickers!
She's racing out of the room!
She's racing upstairs!
Matthew's right behind her!
There's a fight on the landing!
There's a scramble at the bathroom door!

It's Penny! It's Matthew! It's . . .
Splash! They're both in the bath!
But there's a hitch!
Matthew's got soap in his eye!
Penny's got soap up her nose!
They're stalling! But no, they're both fine!

They're both out the bath! They're neck and neck!
It's Matthew! It's Penny! It's Matthew!
Now it's Penny again! She's ahead!
She's first on with her pyjamas!
Now Matthew's catching up! There's nothing in it!

They're climbing into their beds!
Matthew's in the lead with one eye closed!
Now it's Penny again! She's got both closed!
So's Matthew! He's catching up!
It's impossible to tell who's winning!
They're both absolutely quiet!
There's not a murmur from either of them.
It's Matthew! It's Penny! It's . . .
It's a draw! A draw!
But no! Wait a moment! It's not a draw!
Matthew's opened an eye!
He's asking if Penny's asleep yet!
He's disqualified!
So's Penny! She's doing the same!
She's asking if Matthew's asleep yet!
It's impossible! It's daft!
It's the hardest race in the world!

BRIAN PATTEN

AUNTS AND UNCLES

hen Aunty Jane
Became a Crane
She put one leg behind her head;
And even when the clock struck ten
Refused to go to bed.

When Aunty Grace
Became a Plaice
She all but vanished sideways on;
Except her nose
And pointed toes
The rest of her was gone.

When Uncle Grog
Became a Dog
He hid himself for shame;
He sometimes hid his bone as well
And wouldn't hear the front-door bell,
Or answer to his name.

When Aunty Flo
Became a Crow
She had a bed put in a tree;
And there she lay
And read all day
Of ornithology.

When Aunty Vi
Became a Fly
Her favourite nephew
Sought her life;
How could he know
That with each blow
He bruised his Uncle's wife?

When Uncle Sam
Became a Ham
We did not care to carve him up;
He struggled so;
We let him go
And gave him to the pup.

When Aunty Nag
Became a Crag
She stared across the dawn,
To where her spouse
Kept open house
With ladies on the lawn.

When Aunty Mig
Became a Pig
She floated on the briny breeze,
With irritation in her heart
And warts upon her knees.

When Aunty Jill
Became a Pill
She stared all day through dark-blue glass;
And always sneered
When men appeared
To ask her how she was.

When Uncle Jake
Became a Snake
He never found it out;
And so as no one mentions it
One sees him still about.

MERVYN PEAKE

HOMEWORK! OH, HOMEWORK!

omework! Oh, homework!
I hate you! You stink!
I wish I could wash you
away in the sink,
if only a bomb
would explode you to bits.
Homework! Oh, homework!
You're giving me fits.

I'd rather take baths
with a man-eating shark,
or wrestle a lion
alone in the dark,
eat spinach and liver,
pet ten porcupines,
than tackle the homework
my teacher assigns.

Homework! Oh, homework!
You're last on my list,
I simply can't see
why you even exist,
if you just disappeared
it would tickle me pink.
Homework! Oh, homework!
I hate you! You stink!

JACK PRELUTSKY

A MARTIAN SENDS A POSTCARD HOME

Caxtons are mechanical birds with many wings
and some are treasured for their markings –

they cause the eyes to melt
or the body to shriek without pain.

I have never seen one fly, but
sometimes they perch on the hand.

Mist is when the sky is tired of flight
and rests its soft machine on ground:

then the world is dim and bookish
like engravings under tissue paper.

Rain is when the earth is television.
It has the property of making colours darker.

Model T is a room with the lock inside –
a key is turned to free the world

for movement, so quick there is a film
to watch for anything missed.

But time is tied to the wrist
or kept in a box, ticking with impatience.

In homes, a haunted apparatus sleeps,
that snores when you pick it up.

If the ghost cries, they carry it
to their lips and soothe it to sleep

with sounds. And yet, they wake it up
deliberately, by tickling with a finger.

Only the young are allowed to suffer
openly. Adults go to a punishment room

with water but nothing to eat.
They lock the door and suffer the noises

alone. No one is exempt
and everyone's pain has a different smell.

At night, when all the colours die,
they hide in pairs

and read about themselves –
in colour, with their eyelids shut.

CRAIG RAINE

THE SEA

he sea is a hungry dog,
Giant and grey.
He rolls on the beach all day.
With his clashing teeth and shaggy jaws
Hour upon hour he gnaws
The rumbling, tumbling stones,
And 'Bones, bones, bones!'
The giant sea-dog moans,
Licking his greasy paws.

And when the night wind roars
And the moon rocks in the stormy cloud,
He bounds to his feet and snuffs and sniffs,
Shaking his wet sides over the cliffs,
And howls and hollos long and loud.

But on quiet days in May or June,
When even the grasses on the dune
Play no more their reedy tune,
With his head between his paws
He lies on the sandy shores,
So quiet, so quiet, he scarcely snores.

JAMES REEVES

A SPELL FOR SLEEPING

weet william, silverweed, sally-my-handsome.
Dimity darkens the pittering water.
On gloomed lawns wanders a king's daughter.

Curtains are clouding the casement windows.
A moon-glade smurrs the lake with light.
Doves cover the tower with quiet.

Three owls whit-whit in the withies.
Seven fish in a deep pool shimmer.
The princess moves to the spiral stair.

Slowly the sickle moon mounts up.
Frogs hump under moss and mushroom.
The princess climbs to her high hushed room,

Step by step to her shadowed tower.
Water laps the white lake shore.
A ghost opens the princess' door.

> Seven fish in the sway of the water.
> Six candles for a king's daughter.
> Five sighs for a drooping head.
> Four ghosts to gentle her bed.
> Three owls in the dusk falling.
> Two tales to be telling.
> One spell for sleeping.

Tamarisk, trefoil, tormentil.
Sleep rolls down from the clouded hill.
A princess dreams of a silver pool.

The moonlight spreads, the soft ferns flitter.
Stilled in a shimmering drift of water,
Seven fish dream of a lost king's daughter.

ALASTAIR REID

ELETELEPHONY

nce there was an elephant,
Who tried to use the telephant –
No! No! I mean an elephone
Who tried to use the telephone –
(Dear me! I am not certain quite
That even now I've got it right.)

Howe'er it was, he got his trunk
Entangled in the telephunk;
The more he tried to get it free,
The louder buzzed the telephee –
(I fear I'd better drop the song
Of elephop and telephong!)

LAURA E. RICHARDS

IF YOU DON'T PUT YOUR SHOES ON BEFORE I COUNT FIFTEEN

f you don't put your shoes on before I count fifteen
then we won't go to the woods to climb the chestnut
     one
          But I can't find them
Two
          I can't

They're under the sofa three
          No
          O yes
Four five six
          Stop – they've got knots they've got knots

You should untie the laces when you take your shoes
      off seven

                  Will you do one shoe while I do the other then?
Eight but that would be cheating

                  Please

All right

                  It always …
Nine

                  It always sticks – I'll use my teeth
Ten

                  It won't it won't
                  It has – look.
Eleven

                  I'm not wearing any socks
Twelve

                  Stop counting stop counting. Mum where are my socks
                  mum
They're in your shoes. Where you left them.

                  I didn't
Thirteen

                  O they're inside out and upside down and bundled up
Fourteen

                  Have you done the knot on the shoe you were …
Yes
Put it on the right foot

                  But socks don't have right and wrong foot
The shoes silly
Fourteen and a half

                  I am I am. Wait.
                  Don't go to the woods without me
                  Look that's one shoe already
Fourteen and three quarters

                  There

You haven't tied the bows yet
        We could do them on the way there
No we won't fourteen and seven eighths
        Help me then
        You know I'm not fast at bows
Fourteen and fifteen sixteeeeenths
        A single bow is all right isn't it
Fifteen we're off
        See I did it.
        Didn't I?

MICHAEL ROSEN

FLINT

*A*n emerald is as green as grass,
A ruby red as blood;
A sapphire shines as blue as heaven;
A flint lies in the mud.

A diamond is a brilliant stone,
To catch the world's desire;
An opal holds a fiery spark;
But a flint holds fire.

CHRISTINA ROSSETTI

THE VISITOR

 crumbling churchyard, the sea and the moon;
The waves had gouged out grave and bone;
A man was walking, late and alone . . .

 He saw a skeleton on the ground;
A ring on a bony hand he found.

 He ran home to his wife and gave her the ring.
'Oh, where did you get it?' He said not a thing.

 'It's the prettiest ring in the world,' she said,
As it glowed on her finger. They skipped off to bed.

 At midnight they woke. In the dark outside –
'Give me my ring!' a chill voice cried.

 'What was that, William? What did it say?'
'Don't worry, my dear. It'll soon go away.'

'I'm coming!' A skeleton opened the door.
'Give me my ring!' It was crossing the floor.

 'What was that, William? What did it say?'
'Don't worry, my dear. It'll soon go away.'

'I'm reaching you now! I'm climbing the bed.'
The wife pulled the sheet right over her head.

 It was torn from her grasp and tossed in the air:
'I'll drag you out of your bed by the hair!'

'What was that, William? What did it say?'
'Throw the ring through the window! THROW IT AWAY!'

She threw it. The skeleton leapt from the sill,
Scooped up the ring and clattered downhill,
Fainter . . . and fainter . . . Then all was still.

IAN SERRAILLIER

from FOX IN SOCKS

Knox in box.
Fox in socks.

Knox on fox
in socks in box.

Socks on Knox
and Knox in box.

Fox in socks
on box on Knox.

Chicks with bricks come.
Chicks with blocks come.
Chicks with bricks and
blocks and clocks come.

Look, sir. Look, sir.
Mr Knox, sir.
Let's do tricks with
bricks and blocks, sir.
Let's do tricks with
chicks and clocks, sir.

First, I'll make a
quick trick brick stack.
Then I'll make a
quick trick block stack.

You can make a
quick trick chick stack.
You can make a
quick trick clock stack.

And here's a
new trick, Mr Knox. . . .
Socks on chicks
and chicks on fox.
Fox on clocks
on bricks and blocks.
Bricks and blocks
on Knox on box.

DR SEUSS

WITCHES' CHANT *from* Macbeth

ound about the cauldron go:
In the poisoned entrails throw.
Toad, that under cold stone
Days and nights has thirty-one
Sweated venom sleeping got,
Boil thou first in the charmèd pot.
   Double, double toil and trouble;
   Fire burn and cauldron bubble.

Fillet of a fenny snake,
In the cauldron boil and bake;
Eye of newt and toe of frog,
Wool of bat and tongue of dog,
Adder's fork and blindworm's sting,
Lizard's leg and owlet's wing.
For a charm of powerful trouble,
Like a hell-broth boil and bubble.
   Double, double toil and trouble;
   Fire burn and cauldron bubble.

Scale of dragon, tooth of wolf,
Witch's mummy, maw and gulf
Of the ravenous salt-sea shark,
Root of hemlock digged in the dark,
Make the gruel thick and slab:
Add thereto a tiger's chaudron,
For the ingredients of our cauldron.
   Double, double toil and trouble,
   Fire burn and cauldron bubble.

WILLIAM SHAKESPEARE

PENGUIN COMPLAINTS

T he place

    for a penguin

        is clearly

           the fridge.

      It's just

    a bit dark

that's all.

One other

    complaint.

      More fish,

        obviously.

      Your shopping

    list needs

an overhaul.

Furthermore

    there's a

      crowd round

        the ice

      cube tray,

    where polar bears

like to brawl.

But the place

　　　for a penguin

　　　　　has to be

　　　　　　　the fridge,

　　　　　though it's

　　　too small

to sprawl,

if you're tall

　　　you have to crawl

　　　　　and there's

　　　　　　　absolutely

　　　　　nowhere

　　　to lay

an egg.

JO SHAPCOTT

LITTLE ABIGAIL AND THE BEAUTIFUL PONY

 here was a girl named Abigail
Who was taking a drive
Through the country
With her parents
When she spied a beautiful sad-eyed
Grey and white pony.
And next to it was a sign
That said,
FOR SALE – CHEAP.
'Oh,' said Abigail,
'May I have that pony?
May I please?'
And her parents said,
'No you may not.'
And Abigail said,
'But I MUST have that pony.'
And her parents said,
'Well, you can't have that pony,
But you can have a nice butter pecan
Ice cream cone when we get home.'

And Abigail said,
'I don't want a butter pecan
Ice cream cone,
I WANT THAT PONY –
I MUST HAVE THAT PONY.'
And her parents said,
'Be quiet and stop nagging –
You're *not* getting that pony.'
And Abigail began to cry and said,
'If I don't get that pony I'll die.'
And her parents said, 'You won't die.
No child ever died yet from not getting a pony.'
And Abigail felt so bad
That when they got home she went to bed,
And she couldn't eat,
And she couldn't sleep,
And her heart was broken,
And she DID die –
All because of a pony
That her parents wouldn't buy.

(This is a good story
To read to your folks
When they won't buy
You something you want.)

SHEL SILVERSTEIN

JACK FROST IN THE GARDEN

ack Frost was in the garden;
I saw him there at dawn;
He was dancing round the bushes
And prancing on the lawn.
He had a cloak of silver,
A hat all shimm'ring white,
A wand of glittering star-dust,
And shoes of sunbeam light.

Jack Frost was in the garden,
When I went out to play
He nipped my toes and fingers
And quickly ran away.
I chased him round the wood-shed,
But, oh! I'm sad to say
That though I chased him everywhere
He simply wouldn't stay.

Jack Frost was in the garden:
But now I'd like to know
Where I can find him hiding;
I've hunted high and low –
I've lost his cloak of silver,
His hat all shimm'ring white,
His wand of glittering star-dust,
His shoes of sunbeam light.

JOHN P. SMEETON

HOMEWORK

I'm going to do my homework,
As soon as I've had my tea.
I'm going to get on with my homework –
After I've watched T V.

I'll just have a run around the garden,
And then I'll work really hard,
As soon as I've telephoned Jane,
And sent off that birthday card.

I'm going to get on with my homework,
As soon as the rabbits are fed.
I'm going to get on with my homework,
Before it is time for bed.

What! Bedtime already? It can't be –
To get all those good marks I planned,
I simply must do my homework!
Oh Mummy! You don't understand!

ELIZABETH SMITH

I CAN'T FIND MY TEDDY BEAR!

 can't find my teddy bear,
any place, *anywhere*!

Sometimes,
he's inside Mum's sewing box,
darning and mending his woolly socks.

But not today!

Sometimes,
he can be found in our washing machine,
spinning around, trying to get clean.

But not today!

Sometimes,
he sits on top of Dad's chair,
then tumbles down as if for a dare.

But not today!

Sometimes,
when the weather is sunny and fine,
he swings around on the washing line.

But not today!

And sometimes,
he zooms by on a roller skate,
flashing past at such a rate!

But *definitely* not today!

But as the day runs out of light
and the sky turns on the night,
I find him, *at last*, in the best place to be,
propped up on my bed just waiting for me!

IAN SOUTER

FROM A RAILWAY CARRIAGE

Faster than fairies, faster than witches,
Bridges and houses, hedges and ditches,
And charging along like troops in a battle,
All through the meadows the horses and cattle:
All of the sights of the hill and the plain
Fly as thick as driving rain;
And ever again, in the wink of an eye,
Painted stations whistle by.

Here is a child who clambers and scrambles,
All by himself and gathering brambles;
Here is a tramp who stands and gazes;
And there is the green for stringing the daisies!
Here is a cart run away in the road,
Lumping along with man and load;
And here is a mill, and there is a river;
Each a glimpse and gone for ever!

ROBERT LOUIS STEVENSON

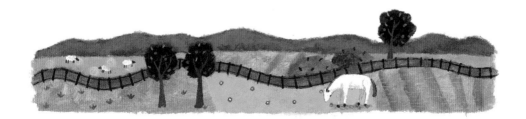

DOG IN SPACE

The barking in space
has died out now,
though dogbones rattle.
And the marks of teeth
on the sputnik's hull
are proof of a battle
impossible to win.

And asteroid-dents
were no help at all.
Did the dog see,
through the window,
earth's blue ball?
Did the dog know
that no other dog
had made that circle
around the earth –
her historic spin
that turned eternal?

MATTHEW SWEENEY

A RIDDLE

We are little airy Creatures,
All of different Voice and Features,
One of us in Glass is set,
One of us you'll find in Jet,
T'other you may see in Tin,
And the fourth a Box within,
If the fifth you shou'd pursue
It can never fly from you.

JONATHAN SWIFT

THE STARS AT NIGHT

winkle, twinkle, little star,
How I wonder what you are!
Up above the world so high,
Like a diamond in the sky.

In the dark blue sky you keep
And often through my curtain peep,
For you never shut your eye
Till the sun is in the sky.

As your bright and tiny spark
Lights the traveller in the dark,
Though I know not what you are,
Twinkle, twinkle, little star.

JANE AND ANN TAYLOR

THE LADY OF SHALOTT

I

n either side the river lie
Long fields of barley and of rye,
That clothe the wold and meet the sky;
And thro' the field the road runs by
    To many-tower'd Camelot;
And up and down the people go,
Gazing where the lilies blow
Round an island there below,
    The island of Shalott.

Willows whiten, aspens quiver,
Little breezes dusk and shiver
Thro' the wave that runs for ever
By the island in the river
    Flowing down to Camelot.
Four gray walls, and four gray towers,
Overlook a space of flowers,
And the silent isle imbowers
    The Lady of Shalott.

By the margin, willow-veil'd,
Slide the heavy barges trail'd
By slow horses; and unhail'd
The shallop flitteth silken-sail'd
    Skimming down to Camelot:
But who hath seen her wave her hand?
Or at the casement seen her stand?
Or is she known in all the land,
    The Lady of Shalott?

Only reapers, reaping early
In among the bearded barley,

Hear a song that echoes cheerly
From the river winding clearly,
   Down to tower'd Camelot;
And by the moon the reaper weary,
Piling sheaves in uplands airy,
Listening, whispers ''Tis the fairy
   Lady of Shalott.'

II
There she weaves by night and day
A magic web with colours gay.
She has heard a whisper say,
A curse is on her if she stay
   To look down to Camelot.
She knows not what the curse may be,
And so she weaveth steadily,
And little other care hath she,
   The Lady of Shalott.

And moving thro' a mirror clear
That hangs before her all the year,
Shadows of the world appear.
There she sees the highway near
   Winding down to Camelot:
There the river eddy whirls,
And there the surly village-churls,
And the red cloaks of market girls,
   Pass onward from Shalott.

Sometimes a troop of damsels glad,
An abbot on an ambling pad,
Sometimes a curly shepherd-lad,
Or long-hair'd page in crimson clad,
   Goes by to tower'd Camelot;

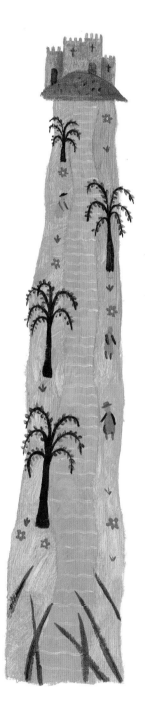

And sometimes thro' the mirror blue
The knights come riding two and two:
She hath no loyal knight and true,
   The Lady of Shalott.

But in her web she still delights
To weave the mirror's magic sights,
For often thro' the silent nights
A funeral, with plumes and lights,
   And music, went to Camelot:
Or when the moon was overhead,
Came two young lovers lately wed;
'I am half sick of shadows,' said
   The Lady of Shalott.

III

A bow-shot from her bower-eaves,
He rode between the barley-sheaves,
The sun came dazzling thro' the leaves,
And flamed upon the brazen greaves
   Of bold Sir Lancelot.
A red-cross knight for ever kneel'd
To a lady in his shield,
That sparkled on the yellow field,
   Beside remote Shalott.

The gemmy bridle glitter'd free,
Like to some branch of stars we see
Hung in the golden Galaxy.
The bridle bells rang merrily
   As he rode down to Camelot:
And from his blazon'd baldric slung
A mighty silver bugle hung,
And as he rode his armour rung,
   Beside remote Shalott.

All in the blue unclouded weather
Thick-jewell'd shone the saddle-leather,
The helmet and the helmet-feather
Burn'd like one burning flame together,
    As he rode down to Camelot.
As often thro' the purple night,
Below the starry clusters bright,
Some bearded meteor, trailing light,
    Moves over still Shalott.

His broad clear brow in sunlight glow'd;
On burnish'd hooves his war-horse trode;
From underneath his helmet flow'd
His coal-black curls as on he rode,
    As he rode down to Camelot.
From the bank and from the river
He flash'd into the crystal mirror,
'Tirra lirra,' by the river
    Sang Sir Lancelot.

She left the web, she left the loom,
She made three paces thro' the room,
She saw the water-lily bloom.
She saw the helmet and the plume,
    She look'd down to Camelot.
Out flew the web and floated wide;
The mirror crack'd from side to side;
'The curse is come upon me!' cried
    The Lady of Shalott.

IV
In the stormy east-wind straining,
The pale yellow woods were waning,
The broad stream in his banks complaining,
Heavily the low sky raining

Over tower'd Camelot;
Down she came and found a boat
Beneath the willow left afloat,
And round about the prow she wrote
    The Lady of Shalott.

And down the river's dim expanse –
Like some bold seer in a trance,
Seeing all his own mischance –
With a glassy countenance
    Did she look to Camelot.
And at the closing of the day,
She loosed the chain, and down she lay;
The broad stream bore her far away,
    The Lady of Shalott.

Lying, robed in snowy white
That loosely flew to left and right –
The leaves upon her falling light –
Thro' the noises of the night
    She floated down to Camelot:
And as the boat-head wound along
The willowy hills and fields among,
They heard her singing her last song,
    The Lady of Shalott.

Heard a carol, mournful, holy,
Chanted loudly, chanted lowly,
Till her blood was frozen slowly,
And her eyes were darken'd wholly,
    Turn'd to tower'd Camelot;

For ere she reach'd upon the tide
The first house by the water-side,
Singing in her song she died,
   The Lady of Shalott.

Under tower and balcony,
By garden wall and gallery,
A gleaming shape she floated by,
Dead-pale between the houses high,
   Silent into Camelot.
Out upon the wharfs they came,
Knight and burgher, lord and dame,
And round the prow they read her name,
   The Lady of Shalott.

Who is this? and what is here?
And in the lighted palace near
Died the sound of royal cheer;
And they cross'd themselves for fear,
   All the Knights at Camelot:
But Lancelot mused a little space;
He said, 'She has a lovely face;
God in His mercy lend her grace,
   The Lady of Shalott.'

ALFRED, LORD TENNYSON

OCTOBER

The green elm with the one great bough of gold
Lets leaves into the grass slip, one by one, –
The short hill grass, the mushrooms small milk-
   white,
Harebell and scabious and tormentil,
That blackberry and gorse, in dew and sun,
Bow down to; and the wind travels too light
To shake the fallen birch leaves from the fern;
The gossamers wander at their own will.
At heavier steps than birds' the squirrels scold.
The rich scene has grown fresh again and new
As Spring and to the touch is not more cool
Than it is warm to the gaze; and now I might
As happy be as earth is beautiful,
Were I some other or with earth could turn
In alternation of violet and rose,
Harebell and snowdrop, at their season due,
And gorse that has no time not to be gay.
But if this be not happiness, – who knows?
Some day I shall think this a happy day,
And this mood by the name of melancholy
Shall no more blackened and obscured be.

EDWARD THOMAS

A DRAGON IN THE CLASSROOM

 There's a dragon in the classroom:
its body is a box,
its head's a plastic waste-bin,
its eyes are broken clocks,

its legs are cardboard tubes,
its claws are toilet rolls,
its tongue's my dad's old tie
(that's why it's full of holes).

'Oh, what a lovely dragon,'
our teacher smiled and said.
'You *are* a pretty dragon,'
she laughed and stroked its head.

'Oh no, I'm not,' he snorted,
SNAP! SNAP! he moved his jaw
and chased our screaming teacher
along the corridor.

CHARLES THOMSON

FAR OVER THE MISTY MOUNTAINS

ar over the misty mountains cold
To dungeons deep and caverns old
We must away ere break of day
To seek the pale enchanted gold.

The dwarves of yore made mighty spells,
While hammers fell like ringing bells
In places deep, where dark things sleep,
In hollow halls beneath the fells.

For ancient king and elvish lord
There many a gleaming golden hoard
They shaped and wrought, and light they caught
To hide in gems on hilt of sword.

On silver necklaces they strung
The flowering stars, on crowns they hung
The dragon-fire, in twisted wire
They meshed the light of moon and sun.

Far over the misty mountains cold
To dungeons deep and caverns old
We must away, ere break of day,
To claim our long-forgotten gold.

Goblets they carved there for themselves
And harps of gold; where no man delves
There lay they long, and many a song
Was sung unheard by men or elves.

The pines were roaring on the height,
The winds were moaning in the night.
The fire was red, it flaming spread;
The trees like torches blazed with light.

The bells were ringing in the dale
And men looked up with faces pale;
The dragon's ire more fierce than fire
Laid low their towers and houses frail.

The mountains smoked beneath the moon;
The dwarves, they heard the tramp of doom.
They fled their hall to dying fall
Beneath his feet, beneath the moon.

Far over the misty mountains grim
To dungeons deep and caverns dim
We must away, ere break of day,
To win our harps and gold from him!

J. R. R. TOLKIEN

THE HAIRY TOE

nce there was a woman went out to pick beans,
and she found a Hairy Toe.
She took the Hairy Toe home with her,
and that night, when she went to bed,
the wind began to moan and groan.
Away off in the distance
she seemed to hear a voice crying,
'Where's my Hair-r-ry To-o-oe?
Who's got my Hair-r-ry To-o-oe?'

The woman scrooched down,
'way down under the covers,
and about that time
the wind appeared to hit the house,

smoosh,

and the old house creaked and cracked
like something was trying to get in.
The voice had come nearer,
almost at the door now,
and it said,
'Where's my Hair-r-ry To-o-oe?
Who's got my Hair-r-ry To-o-oe?'

The woman scrooched further down
under the covers
and pulled them tight around her head.

The wind growled around the house
like some big animal
and r-r-um-mbled
over the chimbley.
All at once she heard the door cr-r-a-ack
and Something slipped in
and began to creep over the floor.

The floor went
cre-e-eak, cre-e-eak
at every step that thing took towards her bed.
The woman could almost feel
it bending over her bed.
There in an awful voice it said:
'Where's my Hair-r-ry To-o-oe?
Who's got my Hair-r-ry To-o-oe?
You've got it!'

TRADITIONAL

THE DAY I FELL DOWN THE TOILET

he day I fell down the toilet
Is a day I'll never forget,
One moment I was in comfort
The next I was helpless and wet.

My feet tipped up to the ceiling
My body collapsed in the bowl,
In haste I grabbed at the handle
And found myself flushed down a hole.

One wave goodbye to the bathroom
And I was lost in the sewer,
Travelling tunnels and caverns
On a raft made out of manure.

Then came the washing-up water
With bits of spaghetti and peas,
The filth from a local factory
And an undiscovered disease.

Drifting along in the darkness,
There was nothing to do but wait.
What would I say to my mum now?
What was it that made me so late?

Suddenly it was all over,
From the end of a pipe I shot
Into a part of the ocean
Where the rubbish was sent to rot.

Glad to escape from the tunnel
To leave all pollution behind,
I found a nice spot on the beach
Then started to bathe and unwind.

But bad things began to pursue me
They stuck to my feet and my hand,
Wreckage was surfing the wave tops
And oil lay around on the sand.

I figured the sewer was safer
For no one said sewers were clean,
I found the pipe that I came from
And waded my way back upstream.

When I got home I was shattered,
I was filthy, ragged and wet,
Rattling the bathroom door was Dad
Saying, 'You off that toilet yet?'

STEVE TURNER

WHEN BETTY EATS SPAGHETTI

 hen Betty eats spaghetti,
She slurps, she slurps, she slurps.
And when she's finished slurping,
She burps, she burps, she burps.

COLIN WEST

THE GRATEFUL DRAGON

A dragon crawled to the castle door
    and everyone inside
looked down on it from the castle walls,
    curious but terrified.

It was half the size of a football pitch,
    bright green, with spots of red,
but it hadn't the strength to lash its tail
    and lay there, as if dead.

The Winter had turned the woods to iron,
    the snow was deep as a house;
there wasn't a blade of grass to be seen
    nor a skinny harvest mouse.

'It's starving!' the King cried. 'Now's our chance!' –
    looking down from the castle wall –
'Bring lances and crossbows and arrows
    and let's kill it, once for all.'

The dragon was too weak to move
    more than an eyelid, and yet
the Princess saw a tear form there and it
    moved her heart with regret.

'Please spare the dragon!' the Princess begged.
　'Put out some bundles of hay.
Once it's grown strong from eating it will
　harmlessly go away.'

The King looked hard in his daughter's face
　and saw how much she cared,
then nodded that they should do as she asked,
　and so the dragon was spared.

Next Autumn brought enemy soldiers.
　The King and his subjects shut
themselves in the castle, and there they starved
　while the harvest stayed uncut.

The Princess wept on the castle wall
　when suddenly there came
in a whirlwind of thunder and fury
　the dragon, spouting flame.

The enemy soldiers ran off in fright
　and never again were seen;
and the people came out of the castle
　and gathered the harvest in.

RAYMOND WILSON

THE DAFFODILS

I wandered lonely as a cloud
That floats on high o'er vales and hills,
When all at once I saw a crowd,
A host, of golden daffodils;
Beside the lake, beneath the trees,
Fluttering and dancing in the breeze.

Continuous as the stars that shine
And twinkle on the Milky Way,
They stretched in never-ending line
Along the margin of a bay:
Ten thousand saw I at a glance,
Tossing their heads in sprightly dance.

The waves beside them danced; but they
Out-did the sparkling waves in glee:
A poet could not but be gay
In such a jocund company:
I gazed – and gazed – but little thought
What wealth to me the show had brought:

For oft, when on my couch I lie
In vacant or in pensive mood,
They flash upon that inward eye
Which is the bliss of solitude;
And then my heart with pleasure fills,
And dances with the daffodils.

WILLIAM WORDSWORTH

THE MAGIC BOX

 I will put in the box

the swish of a silk sari on a summer night,
fire from the nostrils of a Chinese dragon,
the tip of a tongue touching a tooth.

I will put in the box

a snowman with a rumbling belly,
a sip of the bluest water from Lake Lucerne,
a leaping spark from an electric fish.

I will put in the box

three violet wishes spoken in Gujarati,
the last joke of an ancient uncle
and the first smile of a baby.

I will put in the box

a fifth season and a black sun,
a cowboy on a broomstick
and a witch on a white horse.

My box is fashioned from ice and gold and steel,
with stars on the lid and secrets in the corners.
Its hinges are the toe joints
of dinosaurs.

I shall surf on my box
on the great high-rolling breaks of the wild Atlantic,
then wash ashore on a yellow beach
the colour of the sun.

KIT WRIGHT

127

THE FEAR

ow often I turn round
To face the beast that bound by bound
Leaps on me from behind,
Only to see a bough that heaves
With sudden gust of wind
Or blackbird raking withered leaves.

A dog may find me out
Or badger toss a white-lined snout;
And one day as I softly trod
Looking for nothing stranger than
A fox or stoat I met a man
And even that seemed not too odd.

And yet in any place I go
I watch and listen as all creatures do
For what I cannot see or hear,
For something warns me everywhere
That even in my land of birth
I trespass the earth.

ANDREW YOUNG

LITTLE SISTER

That's my little sister
Just five minutes old
Already seeking something
To bite and chew and hold,
That's my little sister
Already going bald
I can't just call her sister
So what will she be called?

When I hear her crying
I want to call her *loud*
If she's the type for talking
I may call her a *crowd*,
If she's good at singing
I'll call her *nightingale*
If she keeps on grinning
She'll make the doctors wail.

I want to call her Carol
But all carols are hymns
I want to call her Jimmy
But I always visit gyms,
I want to call her spotty
But she may punch my nose
I will not call her Rosy
She don't look like a rose.

The doctors called her beauty
But beauty is a horse
The nurses called her cutey
Being polite of course,
My Mummy and my Daddy
Just don't have an idea
We don't have a name ready
But we're so glad she's here.

BENJAMIN ZEPHANIAH

INDEX OF FIRST LINES

CONTRIBUTING SCHOOLS

Puffin Books would like to thank the following schools for their help in choosing *100 Best Poems for Children*:

Alderley Edge School for Girls, Alderley Edge, Cheshire
All Souls C. E., Rye St Heywood, Lancashire
Arnold Lodge School, Leamington Spa, Warwickshire
Ash Field School, Leicester, Leicestershire
Auchenblae School, Laurencekirk, Aberdeenshire
Avebury Primary School, Marlborough, Wiltshire
Bailey Green First School, Killingworth, Tyne and Wear
Baines Endowed C. E. (Aided) Primary, Blackpool, Lancashire
Ballycarry Primary School, Carrickfergus, County Antrim
Ballyholme Primary School, Bangor, County Down
Ballymoney Model Primary School, Ballymoney, County Antrim
Ballyroan Boys National School, Dublin
Bedford High School, Bedford, Bedfordshire
Beechlawn, Hillsborough, County Down
Bewbush Middle School, Crawley, Surrey
Bignold Middle School, Norwich, Norfolk
Birkenhead Preparatory School, Birkenhead, Merseyside
Bishop of Llandaff C/W High School, Llandaff, Cardiff
Brampton Junior School, Chesterfield, Derbyshire
Broadway Primary School, Rossendale, Lancashire
Cardinham School, Bodmin, Cornwall
Cartmel Priory School, Grange-o-Sands, Cumbria
Castlefields Primary School, Bridgnorth, Shropshire
Chandlers Field School, West Molesey, Surrey
Charterhouse Square School, London
Charters School, Sunningdale, Berkshire

Checkendon Primary School, Reading, Berkshire
Chislehurst C. E. Primary School, Chislehurst, Kent
Churchfields Primary School, Beckenham, Kent
Clogher Valley Independent Christian School, Fivemiletown, County Tyrone
Clough Primary School, Downpatrick, County Down
Coole National School, Mullingar, County Westmeath
Cornholme J & I School, Todmorden, Lancashire
Corpus Christi College, Belfast, County Antrim
Corpus Christi R. C. Primary School, Oldham, Lancashire
Corran Integrated Primary, Larne, Belfast, County Antrim
Daisyfield Primary School, Blackburn, Lancashire
Derby High School, Bury, Lancashire
Ely St John's Primary, Ely, Cambridgeshire
Fairfield School, Bristol, Avon
Farnborough School, Clifton, Nottinghamshire
Ferrars Junior School, Luton, Bedfordshire
Fishbourne Church of England Primary, Chichester, West Sussex
Flintham Primary School, Newark, Nottinghamshire
Frederick Gough School, Scunthorpe, North Lincolnshire
Friern Barnet School, London
Gatehouse School, London
Gloucester Islamic Secondary School, Gloucester, Gloucestershire
Great Alne Primary, Nr. Alcester, Warwickshire
Groggan Primary School, Randalstown, County Antrim
Harrold Priory Middle School, Harrold, Bedfordshire
Hartford High School, Northwich, Cheshire
Hasbury Primary, Halesowen, West Midlands
Hazlegrove House School, Yeovil, Somerset
Heycroft Primary School, Leigh-on-Sea, Essex
Hillgrove School, Bangor, Gwynedd
Hindsford Primary School, Atherton, Greater Manchester
Holt Farm Primary School, Halesowen, West Midlands
Kewl Bank C. E., Ripon, North Yorkshire
Kilcooley Primary School, Bangor, County Down
Laneshawbridge Primary School, Colne, Lancashire
Langley Juniors, Southway, Devon
Leonard Stanley C of E School, Leonard Stanley, Gloucestershire

Lilleshall Primary School, Newport, Shropshire

Lisfearty Primary School, Dungannon,
County Tyrone

Lisnasharragh Primary, Cregagh, Belfast

Lowther Endowed School, Penrith, Cumbria

Lurgan Model Primary School, Lurgan,
County Armagh

Lyndhurst School, Camberley, Surrey

Manor Leas Junior School, Lincoln, Lincolnshire

Marton County Primary School, Blackpool,
Lancashire

Mayfield Preparatory School, Walsall, West Midlands

Meoncross, Fareham, Hampshire

Merdon Junior School, Eastleigh, Hampshire

Mersey Street Primary, Belfast

Mullagh Central National School, Kells,
County Meath

New College Leicester, Leicester, Leicestershire

Oakleigh House School, Swansea, West Glamorgan

Our Lady & St Anselm R. C. School, Whitworth,
Lancashire

Parrett and Axe C. E., V. A. Primary School,
Beaminster, Dorset

Piercestown National School, Piercestown,
County Wexford

Ratoath National School, Ratoath, County Neath

Read St John's C. E. Primary School, Burnley,
Lancashire

Redhill Primary School, Ockbrook, Derbyshire

Roman Way First School, Redditch, West Midlands

Roydon C. P. School, Diss, Norfolk

S. N. Abban, Via Carlow, County Laois

St Alfege with St Peter's, London

St Angela's Ursuline School, London

St Anne's Primary School, Derry

St Anthony's Primary School, Craigavon,
County Armagh

St Attracta's Senior School, Meadowbrook, Dublin

St Benedict's Junior School, London

St Chad's R.C. Primary School, London

St Laurence's N. S., Athy, County Kildare

St Luke's School, Douglas, County Cork

St Mary Abbots School, London

St Mary and St John C. E.V. A Primary School,
Rutland, Leicestershire

St Mary's N. S., Lifford, County Donegal

St Oliver Plunkett's Primary School, Kilmore,
County Armagh

St Patrick's Primary School, Tuam, County Galway

St Peter's C of E Primary, Chelmsford, Essex

St Petroc's Ceva Primary, Bodmin, Cornwall

St Wilfrid's R.C. High School, Castleford,
West Yorkshire

Saxon Wood School, Basingstoke, Hampshire

Scoil Ioságaín, Buncrana, County Donegal

Scoill Phurt le Moirrey, St Mary, Isle of Man

Skerton High School, Lancaster, Lancashire

South Milford Community Primary, South Milford,
West Yorkshire

Stainburn School, Workington, Cumbria

Stanley Park Juniors, Carshalton, Surrey

Steeple Morden C. E. Primary, Royston,
Hertfordshire

Stourfield Junior, Bournemouth, Dorset

Summerhill, Kingswinford, West Midlands

Swithland St Leonard's C. E. Primary,
Loughborough, Leicestershire

The Cathedral School, Llandaff, Cardiff

The Chandler C. of E. Junior School, Godalming,
Surrey

The Gilberd School, Colchester, Essex

The King Edmund School, Rochford, Essex

The King's Junior School, Worcester, Worcestershire

The Meadow, Bordon, Hampshire

Waverley House P. N. E. U. School, Nottingham,
Nottinghamshire

Welford-on-Avon Primary School,
Stratford-upon-Avon, Warwickshire

Westcott Primary, Hull, East Yorkshire

Westley Middle School, Bury St Edmunds, Suffolk

Whitburn School, South Tyneside, Tyne and Wear

Whittington Grange School, Lichfield, Staffordshire

Wimbledon Chase Middle School, London

Wimborne First School, Wimborne, Dorset

Woodlands Junior School, Tonbridge, Kent

Yarborough School, Lincoln, Lincolnshire

Yarmouth C.E. Primary School, Yarmouth,
Isle of Wight

Yorston Lodge School, Knutsford, Cheshire

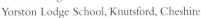

ACKNOWLEDGEMENTS

The publishers gratefully acknowledge the following for permission to reproduce copyright material.
Every effort has been made to trace copyright holders, but in some cases has proved impossible. The publishers
would be happy to hear from any copyright holder that has not been acknowledged.

'What Turkey Doing?' by John Agard from *No Hickory, No Dickory, No Dock*, published by Viking 1991, reprinted by kind permission of John Agard c/o Caroline Sheldon Literary Agency copyright © John Agard, 1991; 'Please Mrs Butler' by Allan Ahlberg from *Please Mrs Butler*, published by Kestrel 1983, copyright © Allan Ahlberg, 1983, reprinted by permission of Penguin Books Ltd; 'November Night Countdown' by Moira Andrew, from *Rhymes about the Year* edited by John Foster, published by OUP 1999, copyright © Moira Andrew, 1999, reprinted by kind permission of the author; 'Song of the Worms' by Margaret Atwood, from *Poems 1965–1975*, reprinted by permission of Little Brown, UK; 'The Dolly on the Dustcart' by Pam Ayres, from *Some More of Me Poetry*, reprinted by permission of Sheil Land Associates Ltd; 'Matilda' by Hillaire Belloc, from *Cautionary Verses,* published by Random House UK, copyright © Hillaire Belloc, reprinted by permission of Peters Fraser & Dunlop on behalf of Hillaire Belloc; 'Starter' by Tony Bradman, from *Smile Please*, published by Viking Kestrel, copyright © Tony Bradman, 1987, reprinted by permission of Penguin Books Ltd; 'November Evening' by Gerald Bullett, from *News from the Village*, copyright © Gerald Bullett 1951, reprinted by permission of Peters Fraser & Dunlop on behalf of the Estate of Gerald Bullett; 'Colonel Fazackerley' by Charles Causley, from *Figgie Hobbin*, published by Macmillan, reprinted by permission of David Higham Associates Limited; 'I Think My Teacher Is A Cowboy' by John Coldwell, copyright © John Coldwell, reprinted by permission of the author; 'Kenneth' by Wendy Cope, copyright © Wendy Cope, reprinted by permission of the author; 'Little Red Riding Wolf' by Roald Dahl, from *Revolting Rhymes*, published by Jonathan Cape, reprinted by permission of The Random House Group Limited; 'The Listeners' by Walter de la Mare, from *The Complete Poems of Walter de la Mare, 1969*, reprinted by permission of The Literary Trustees of Walter de la Mare, and the Society of Authors as their representatives; 'Please Sir' by Peter Dixon, published by Peche Luna, copyright © Peter Dixon, reprinted by kind permission of the author; 'The Bird's Nest' by John Drinkwater, reprinted by kind permission of Samuel French Limited on behalf of the Estate of John Drinkwater; 'The Word Party' by Richard Edwards, from *The Word Party*, published by Lutterworth Press, reprinted by permission of the author; 'Macavity: The Mystery Cat' by T. S. Eliot, from *Old Possum's Book of Practical Cats*, published by Faber and Faber, reprinted by permission of Faber and Faber Limited; 'Water Voles and Moles' by Gavin Ewart, from *Caterpillar Stew*, published by Red Fox, 1990, reprinted by permission of Mrs M. A. Ewart; 'Cats' by Eleanor Farjeon, from *The Children's Bells*, published by OUP, reprinted by permission of David Higham Associates Limited; 'Four o'Clock Friday' by John Foster, from *Four o'Clock Friday*, published by OUP, copyright © John Foster 1991, reprinted by kind